中外文稀有版本文献

《德国的革命和反革命》

英文版

【德】弗里德里希·恩格斯 ◎ 著

图书在版编目（CIP）数据

《德国的革命和反革命》中外文稀有版本文献：德文、英文、汉文 /（德）弗里德里希·恩格斯著；柯柏年等译 . —— 北京：中央编译出版社，2024.6
ISBN 978-7-5117-4753-2

Ⅰ.①德… Ⅱ.①弗… ②柯… Ⅲ.①恩格斯著作—单行本— 1885 —德、英、汉 Ⅳ.① A122

中国国家版本馆 CIP 数据核字 (2024) 第 092669 号

《德国的革命和反革命》中外文稀有版本文献

策划统筹	张远航
责任编辑	郑永杰　宋　妍
责任印制	李　颖
出版发行	中央编译出版社
网　　址	www.cctpcm.com
地　　址	北京市海淀区北四环西路 69 号（100080）
电　　话	（010）55627391（总编室）　（010）55627319（编辑室）
	（010）55627320（发行部）　（010）55627377（新技术部）
经　　销	全国新华书店
印　　刷	廊坊市印艺阁数字科技有限公司
开　　本	710 毫米 ×1000 毫米 1/16
字　　数	590 千字
印　　张	50.75
版　　次	2024 年 6 月第 1 版
印　　次	2024 年 6 月第 1 次印刷
定　　价	1980.00 元（全 4 册）

新浪微博：@中央编译出版社　　　　微　信：中央编译出版社（ID：cctphome）
淘宝店铺：中央编译出版社直销店（http://shop108367160.taobao.com）（010）55627331

本社常年法律顾问：北京市吴栾赵阎律师事务所律师　闫军　梁勤
凡有印装质量问题，本社负责调换，电话：（010）55627320

前　言

《德国的革命和反革命》是恩格斯总结德国1848—1849年革命经验的重要著作。恩格斯指出应该根据社会总的经济状况和生活条件研究革命发生和成败的原因，他论述了无产阶级领导权和工农联盟的问题，他强调革命是"社会进步和政治进步的强大推动力"，阐明了无产阶级革命斗争的策略原则。

《德国的革命和反革命》原文是恩格斯1851年8月—1852年9月写的19篇文章。1851年7月底，《纽约每日论坛报》编辑查·德纳约请马克思为该报撰稿，由于马克思忙于经济学研究，因此请恩格斯帮忙撰写了这些文章。这些文章发表在《纽约每日论坛报》的"德国"专栏，署名为"卡·马克思"，直到1913年马克思和恩格斯的来往书信发表后，人们才知道作者是恩格斯。这组文章在马克思、恩格斯生前没有出版过单行本，只有开头的几篇曾被译成德文在美国的德文报纸《纽约晚报》以及柏林出版的《德意志总汇报》上转载过。1896年，马克思的小女儿爱琳娜用原文字（英文）对这组文章进行编辑，于同年4月在英国出版单行本，书名为《革命和反革命或1848年的德国》。1900年，马克思的二女儿劳拉将此书译成法文出版。

《德国的革命和反革命》首个中文全译本1930年5月由上海新生命书局出版，译者是刘镜园，书名译为《革命与反革命》。译者指出，该译本是根据卡·考茨基1896年翻译出版的德文本和当时在苏联出版的俄文单行本翻译的。这个译本在新生命书局先后三次再版。第二个中文全

1

译本由王右铭、柯柏年翻译，1939年3月上海生活书店出版，这是中国共产党直接组织翻译及出版的第一个中文全译本。1939年4月，这个译本作为"马恩丛书"第八种在延安解放社重印，译文、版式等均未变动，但译者改为王石巍、柯柏年。该译本先后在解放社、新华书店等机构多次重印。

中华人民共和国成立后，由中央编译局翻译的《德国的革命和反革命》新译本最早于1961年出版，收入《马克思恩格斯全集》第八卷。此后，市面流通的版本基本为中央编译局译本。为向国内学者提供权威的版本资料，进一步推动《德国的革命和反革命》的研究，中央编译出版社此次整理出版了《德国的革命和反革命》在全世界传播较为广泛的英文版、德文版，以及1949年前中国出版的全译本。如有不当之处，敬请批评指正。

张远航

2024年3月

MARXIST LIBRARY
VOLUME XIII

GERMANY:
REVOLUTION AND
COUNTER-REVOLUTION

FREDERICK ENGELS

MARXIST LIBRARY

Works of Marxism-Leninism

Germany: Revolution and Counter-Revolution

MARXIST LIBRARY
Works of Marxism—Leninism
VOLUME XIII

GERMANY: REVOLUTION AND COUNTER-REVOLUTION

By FREDERICK ENGELS

NEW YORK
INTERNATIONAL PUBLISHERS

All Rights Reserved

1933
PRINTED IN ENGLAND BY
THE GARDEN CITY PRESS LIMITED
LETCHWORTH, HERTS
(T.U. IN ALL DEPARTMENTS)

CONTENTS

	PAGE
EDITOR'S PREFACE	3
CHAPTER I	9
II	18
III	28
IV	33
V	40
VI	44
VII	49
VIII	54
IX	58
X	62
XI	66
XII	72
XIII	80
XIV	85
XV	90
XVI	94
XVII	98
XVIII	103
XIX	108
XX THE LATE TRIAL AT COLOGNE	114
APPENDIX 1. HISTORY OF THE COMMUNIST LEAGUE	120
APPENDIX 2. DEMANDS OF THE COMMUNIST PARTY IN GERMANY	132
APPENDIX 3. FIRST ADDRESS OF THE CENTRAL COMMITTEE OF THE COMMUNIST LEAGUE TO ITS MEMBERS IN GERMANY	135
GLOSSARY OF NAMES AND PHRASES	147

PREFACE

MARX was asked in the summer of 1851 to write a series of articles for the *New York Daily Tribune* on the German Revolution. The request came from Dana, the foreign editor, who had met Marx at Cologne during the Revolution and was impressed by him as the most outstanding and authoritative of the leaders of the great revolutionary movement of 1848-9. Marx was busy at the time on his book *Critique of Political Economy* and asked Engels to write them for him. Moreover, at this time he only knew English very imperfectly.

Engels consented, wrote the articles in Manchester and sent them on to Marx to be edited and despatched to New York. Although, therefore, Engels must be rightly considered their author, Marx took a big part in their preparation, for in their almost daily correspondence the chief points were thoroughly discussed between the two. The collaboration in the *New York Tribune* thus begun was continued till 1863, and though Marx himself wrote most of the articles after the end of 1852, when his command of the language allowed it, Engels continued to help and contributed scores of invaluable articles on political and military affairs.

We have included in this edition, in order to give the reader a perfectly clear idea of the tactics of Marx and Engels in the German Revolution, an article by Engels on the history of the Communist League and two documents of the League which are of the greatest importance for understanding the part which it played in the events of 1848-9. Engels' article first appeared in 1885 as the introduction to a reprint of Marx's account of the Cologne Communist Trial. The Demands of the Communist Party in Germany, written by Marx and Engels, were drawn up directly after the first revolutionary outbreaks of the spring of 1848, while the Address of the Central Committee of the League was written by Marx and issued by the League after its members had gathered together in exile in London following the defeat of the revolution.

PREFACE

This book is therefore no abstract historical document, or the calm reflection of academic minds on the events of the past. It is in every sense a revolutionary document, the judgment of two master revolutionaries on their own work. In it Marx and Engels analyse the great popular movement in Germany, mercilessly expose the causes of its failure and explain at the same time the tactic of the proletarian wing of the revolutionary movement. The changes that it was found necessary to make in that tactic are explained in the last document, one of the most important revolutionary documents of all time.

It is a long time since 1848, but it would be foolish to imagine that the events of that year are of no importance to the workers' movement of to-day. Revolution and counter-revolution in Germany are to-day once more in the centre of world history. The problems to be solved and the forces at work are different, but it cannot be denied that had events in 1848 gone as Marx and Engels desired they should go, and worked that they should go, there would be no Fascist dictatorship in Germany to-day, nor would there have been an imperialist war of 1914-18.

The revolution in Germany in 1848 was a democratic one against feudalism. The German workers, the peasantry, the bourgeoisie and petty-bourgeoisie of the towns were united against the reactionary monarchy in Prussia, against the rulers of the other German states. Yet in the course of the revolution the bourgeoisie went over to the reaction, followed by large sections of the petty-bourgeoisie, the peasantry became indifferent or hostile and the working men and a minority of the petty-bourgeoisie were left alone to fight against counter-revolution.

Feudalism was not overthrown in Germany in 1848. The plebeian revolution failed to accomplish the unification of Germany. The foundation of the modern German state was to be undertaken in a different way, by the " blood and iron " dictatorship of Bismarck, by " revolution " from above. Capitalist Germany was founded on a compromise by which the bourgeoisie, in deadly fear of the working class, gave power to the junkers and the militarists, helped in the creation of the non-commissioned officers' paradise of modern Germany.

The failure of 1848 was the triumph of 1871, of the annexation of Alsace-Lorraine and the placing of Germany on the path of imperialist development. In his introduction to the *Civil War in*

PREFACE

France of Marx, Engels prophetically outlines the future which was to result from the failure of 1848 and the consequent triumph of Bismarck:

"And have we not seen the literal fulfilment of the prophecy that the annexation of Alsace-Lorraine would 'drive France into the arms of Russia,' and that after the annexation Germany must either become the avowed tool of Russia, or must, after some short respite, prepare for a new war, and moreover, 'a race war against the Allied Slav and Latin races'? ... And is there not perpetually hanging over our heads the Damocles' sword of another war, on the first day of which all the chartered covenants of princes will be scattered like chaff; a war of which nothing is certain but the absolute uncertainty of what will be its outcome; a race war which will subject the whole of Europe to devastation by fifteen or twenty million armed men, and is only not already raging because even the strongest of the great military States shrinks before the absolute incalculability of its final outcome?"

The outcome of that war for Germany was the incomplete workers' revolution of 1918, betrayed by German Social-Democracy, who have tried to solve the new problems created by the war, the new national question caused by the break-up of the Empire and the terrible exploitation of the people through the Versailles Treaty, in the way chosen by Lassalle after 1848 and bitterly fought by Marx and Engels. That way is the way of support for the dictatorship of German capitalism, ending in final capitulation to Fascism, the new "revolution from above," which, like Bismarck's policy, cannot solve Germany's problems but only complicate them anew.

The problems of Germany in 1848 in the struggle against feudalism were those of almost every country in a similar historical position. Eighteen forty-eight in Germany, 1905-7 in Russia, 1926-7 and after in China, have confronted the workers with the same historical tasks and on the basis of Marx and Engels' tactics in 1848, as outlined in this book, they have approached these tasks and, in part at least, triumphantly fulfilled them.

Marx and Engels in 1848 were the leaders of the German working class, the leaders of the only international workers' party, the Communist League, whose Manifesto, written by them, was published as the smoke was clearing from the first barricades in Paris. The history of the League, given by Engels in the first Appendix, shows clearly that at the end of 1847 the majority of its members were still only approaching the scientific communism of the authors of the Manifesto. The Party was not strong enough to have rallied and led the working class in Germany in the revolution independently of all other parties. So Marx and Engels on their return to Germany were in favour of co-operation with the democratic parties of the left.

In his " Conversation with the Students of the Sun Yat Sen University," Stalin sums up the Marxian tactic in 1848:

" It is not true that Marxism rejects in principle a party composed of a *bloc* of oppressed revolutionary classes, that it is in principle impermissible for Marxists to enter into such a party. . . . In fact Marxism has not only recognised (and continues to recognise) the principle of the permissibility of Marxists entering such a party, but in fact in concrete historical circumstances has carried out such an entrance. I could refer to such an example as that of Marx himself in 1848, during the German Revolution, when Marx and his fellow thinkers entered a well-known bourgeois democratic union in Germany and there co-operated with the representatives of the revolutionary bourgeoisie. It is well known that besides the Marxists the representatives of the revolutionary bourgeoisie also entered that bourgeois-democratic union, that bourgeois-revolutionary party. The *New Rhenish Gazette* which Marx edited then was the organ of the bourgeois-democratic league. Only in the spring of 1849 when the Revolution in Germany began to ebb, did Marx and his fellow thinkers leave the bourgeois-democratic union, having decided to set up a perfectly independent organisation of the working class with an independent class policy."

The break-up of that democratic coalition, the pitiful hesitations and treacheries of the German bourgeoisie, particularly of its " left," petty-bourgeois wing, are brilliantly described in Engels' articles for the *New York Tribune*. One thing stands out absolutely from the book, that the only consistently revolutionary force in Germany (as elsewhere in Europe) was the working class, and

PREFACE

Marx and Engels bent all their efforts to freeing it from the influence of the democrats. " The Proletarian, really Revolutionary Party," writes Engels, " succeeded only very gradually in withdrawing the mass of the working people from the influence of the Democrats, whose tail they formed in the beginning of the Revolution. But in due time the indecision, weakness and cowardice of the Democratic leaders did the rest, and it may now be said to be one of the principle results of the last years' convulsions, that wherever the working class is concerned in anything like considerable masses, they are entirely freed from that democratic influence which led them into an endless series of blunders and misfortunes during 1848 and 1849" (Chap. VI,pp. 47-48).

The fruit of that experience is summed up in the famous address printed here as Appendix III, in which the growth of Marxist ideas, the hope of a new rise of the revolutionary wave in Germany, led Marx to the formulation of the idea of " permanent revolution." It is sufficient to read carefully the articles " Revolution and Counter-Revolution " and then the " Address," to see that Marx and Engels never dreamed for a moment that it was possible in Germany to skip over the phase of the bourgeois revolution. The stress laid upon the importance of the peasantry, the national question (here first treated by them), the insistence on the *democratic* character of the coming revolution (as emphasised in the demands of the Communist Party printed in Appendix II), all prove this.

In dealing with the insurrection of 1849, there is a passage in Chapter XVIII which is here of capital importance:

" The working class entered upon this insurrection as they would have done upon any other which promised either to remove some obstacles in their progress towards political dominion and social revolution, or, at least, to tie the more influential but less courageous class of society to a more decided and revolutionary course than they had followed hitherto. The working class took up arms with a full knowledge that this was, in the direct bearings of the case, no quarrel of its own: but it followed up its only true policy, to allow no class that has risen on its shoulders (as the bourgeoisie had done in 1848) to fortify its class-government without opening, at least, a fair field to the working classes for the struggle of its own interests, and, in any case, to bring matters to a crisis, by which the nation was fairly and irresistibly launched in the revolutionary career, or else the *status quo* before the Revolution restored as nearly as possible, and, thereby, a new revolution rendered unavoidable " (pp. 103-4).

The Menshevik distortion of the tactics of Marx and Engels in the revolution of 1848, was made into a complete theory by Parvus in 1905 and from him adopted by Trotsky. Lenin fought strenuously against the Menshevik distortions of Marx in 1905, striving to guide the Revolution to its first stage of a revolutionary democratic dictatorship of proletariat and peasantry. When in 1917 the Russian masses overthrew the Tsar and set up their own organs of power alongside the bourgeois Provisional Government of Kerensky, Lenin at once called for the turning of this revolution into a socialist uprising, for the handing over of all power to the Soviets as the organ of the dictatorship of the proletariat *in alliance with the poor peasantry*.

In 1905, in 1917, and again in the Chinese Revolution to-day, where the democratic dictatorship of proletariat and peasantry exists in the Soviet regions, Trotsky denied the Marxist tactics of 1848, the Marxist line of the " Address " of 1850, fought bitterly against Lenin's development of the line of Marx and Engels, and for his own opportunist and Menshevik theory of " permanent revolution " which in practice means the supporting of the bourgeois-liberal slogan of the " Constituent Assembly," which attempts to work through such counter-revolutionary bodies as the Kuomintang, instead of, as Marx and Engels did when circumstances temporarily forced them into such a position in 1848, fighting to destroy " democratic " influence over the proletariat, to develop the independent class party of the workers.

We are convinced that not only has history proved Trotsky to be mistaken, and Marx, Engels, Lenin and Stalin right, but that the reading of this book will show that the two great founders of revolutionary, scientific Communism, wrote history in such away that it throws a flood of light on the practical problems of the working class to-day, not only in Germany, but in China, in India, in Spain, wherever the tide of revolutionary conflict is rising and the working class finds its further development hindered by the lumber of the Middle Ages, and where the peasantry, crushed by that same mediæval lumber, is the ally of the working class in the coming revolution.

GERMANY: REVOLUTION AND COUNTER-REVOLUTION

I

London, September 1851.

THE first act of the revolutionary drama on the continent of Europe has closed. The "powers that were" before the hurricane of 1848 are again the "powers that be," and the more or less popular rulers of a day, provisional governors, triumvirs, dictators, with their tail of representatives, civil commissioners, military commissioners, prefects, judges, generals, officers, and soldiers, are thrown upon foreign shores, and "transported beyond the seas" to England or America, there to form new governments *in partibus infidelium*, European committees, central committees, national committees, and to announce their advent with proclamations quite as solemn as those of any less imaginary potentates.

A more signal defeat than that undergone by the continental revolutionary party—or rather parties—upon all points of the line of battle, cannot be imagined. But what of that? Has not the struggle of the British middle classes for their social and political supremacy embraced forty-eight, that of the French middle classes forty, years of unexampled struggles? And was their triumph ever nearer than at the very moment when restored monarchy thought itself more firmly settled than ever? The times of that superstition which attributed revolutions to the ill will of a few agitators have long passed away. Everyone knows nowadays that wherever there is a revolutionary convulsion, there must be some social want in the background, which is prevented, by outworn institutions, from satisfying itself. The want may not yet be felt as strongly, as generally, as might ensure immediate success; but every attempt at forcible repression will only bring it forth stronger and stronger, until it bursts its fetters. If, then, we have been beaten, we have nothing else to do but to begin again from the beginning. And, fortunately, the probably

9

very short interval of rest which is allowed us between the close of the first and the beginning of the second act of the movement, gives us time for a very necessary piece of work: the study of the causes that necessitated both the late outbreak and its defeat; causes that are not to be sought for in the accidental efforts, talents, faults, errors, or treacheries of some of the leaders, but in the general social state and conditions of existence of each of the convulsed nations. That the sudden movements of February and March 1848 were not the work of single individuals, but spontaneous, irresistible manifestations of national wants and necessities, more or less clearly understood, but very distinctly felt by numerous classes in every country, is a fact recognised everywhere; but when you inquire into the causes of the counter-revolutionary successes, there you are met on every hand with the ready reply that it was Mr. This or Citizen That who " betrayed " the people. Which reply may be very true or not, according to circumstances, but under no circumstances does it explain anything—not even show how it came to pass that the " people " allowed themselves to be thus betrayed. And what a poor chance stands a political party whose entire stock-in-trade consists in a knowledge of the solitary fact that Citizen So-and-so is not to be trusted.

The inquiry into, and the exposition of, the causes, both of the revolutionary convulsion and its suppression, are, besides, of paramount importance from an historical point of view. All these petty, personal quarrels and recriminations—all these contradictory assertions that it was Marrast, or Ledru-Rollin, or Louis Blanc, or any other member of the Provisional Government, or the whole of them, that steered the Revolution amidst the rocks upon which it foundered—of what interest can they be, what light can they afford, to the American or Englishman who observed all these various movements from a distance too great to allow of his distinguishing any of the details of operations? No man in his senses will ever believe that eleven men, mostly of very indifferent capacity either for good or evil, were able in three months to ruin a nation of thirty-six millions, unless those thirty-six millions saw as little of their way before them as the eleven did. But how it came to pass that thirty-six millions were at once called upon to decide for themselves which way to go, although partly groping in dim twilight, and how then they got lost and their old leaders were for a moment allowed to return to their leadership, that is just the question.

If, then, we try to lay before the readers of the *Tribune* the causes which, while they necessitated the German Revolution of 1848, led quite as inevitably to its momentary repression in 1849 and 1850, we shall not be expected to give a complete history of events as they passed in that country. Later events, and the judgment of coming generations, will decide what portion of that confused mass of seemingly accidental, incoherent, and incongruous facts is to form a part of the world's history. The time for such a task has not yet arrived; we must confine ourselves to the limits of the possible, and be satisfied, if we can find rational causes, based upon undeniable facts, to explain the chief events, the principal vicissitudes of that movement, and to give us a clue as to the direction which the next, and perhaps not very distant, outbreak will impart to the German people.

And firstly, what was the state of Germany at the outbreak of the Revolution?

The composition of the different classes of the people which form the groundwork of every political organisation was, in Germany, more complicated than in any other country. While in England and France feudalism was entirely destroyed, or, at least, reduced, as in the former country, to a few insignificant forms, by a powerful and wealthy middle class, concentrated in large towns, and particularly in the capital, the feudal nobility in Germany had retained a great portion of their ancient privileges. The feudal system of tenure was prevalent almost everywhere. The lords of the land had even retained the jurisdiction over their tenants. Deprived of their political privileges, of the right to control the princes, they had preserved almost all their mediæval supremacy over the peasantry of their demesnes, as well as their exemption from taxes. Feudalism was more flourishing in some localities than in others, but nowhere except on the left bank of the Rhine was it entirely destroyed. This feudal nobility, then extremely numerous and partly very wealthy, was considered, officially, the first " Order " in the country. It furnished the higher Government officials, it almost exclusively officered the army.

The bourgeoisie of Germany was by far not as wealthy and concentrated as that of France or England. The ancient manufactures of Germany had been destroyed by the introduction of steam, and the rapidly extending supremacy of English manufactures; the more modern manufactures, started under the Napoleonic continental system, established in other parts of the country, did not compensate for the loss of the old ones, nor suffice to create a manufacturing interest strong enough to force its wants upon the notice of Governments jealous of every extension of non-noble wealth and power. If France carried her silk manufactures victorious through fifty years of revolutions and wars, Germany, during the same time, all but lost her ancient linen trade. The manufacturing districts, besides, were few and far between; situated far inland, and using, mostly, foreign, Dutch, or Belgian ports for their imports and exports, they had little or no interest in common with the large seaport towns on the North Sea and the Baltic; they were, above all, unable to create large manufacturing and trading centres, such as Paris and Lyons, London and Manchester. The causes of this backwardness of German manufactures were manifold, but two will suffice to account for it: the unfavourable geographical situation of the country, at a distance from the Atlantic, which had become the great highway for the world's trade, and the continuous wars in which Germany was involved, and which were fought on her soil, from the sixteenth century to the present day. It was this want of numbers, and particularly of anything like concentrated numbers, which prevented the German middle classes from attaining that political supremacy which the English bourgeoisie has enjoyed ever since 1688, and which the French conquered in 1789. And yet, ever since 1815, the wealth, and with the wealth the political importance of the middle class in Germany, was continually growing. Governments were, although reluctantly, compelled to bow, at least to its more immediate material interests. It may even be truly said that from 1815 to 1830, and from 1832 to 1840, every particle of political influence, which, having been allowed to the middle class in the constitutions of the smaller States, was again wrested from them during the above two periods of political reaction, that every such particle was compensated for by some more practical advantage allowed to them. Every political defeat of the middle class drew after it a victory on the field of commercial legislation. And, certainly, the Prussian Protective Tariff of

1818, and the formation of the Zollverein, were worth a good deal more to the traders and manufacturers of Germany than the equivocal right of expressing in the chambers of some diminutive dukedom their want of confidence in ministers who laughed at their votes. Thus, with growing wealth and extending trade, the bourgeoisie soon arrived at a stage where it found the development of its most important interests checked by the political constitution of the country; by its random division among thirty-six princes with conflicting tendencies and caprices; by the feudal fetters upon agriculture and the trade connected with it; by the prying superintendence to which an ignorant and presumptuous bureaucracy subjected all its transactions. At the same time the extension and consolidation of the Zollverein, the general introduction of steam communication, the growing competition in the home trade, brought the commercial classes of the different States and Provinces closer together, equalised their interests, centralised their strength. The natural consequence was the passing of the whole mass of them into the camp of the Liberal Opposition, and the gaining of the first serious struggle of the German middle class for political power. This change may be dated from 1840, from the moment when the bourgeoisie of Prussia assumed the lead of the middle-class movement of Germany. We shall hereafter revert to this Liberal Opposition movement of 1840-7.

The great mass of the nation, which neither belonged to the nobility nor to the bourgeoisie, consisted in the towns of the small trading and shopkeeping class and the working people, and in the country of the peasantry.

The small trading and shopkeeping class is exceedingly numerous in Germany, in consequence of the stinted development which the large capitalists and manufacturers as a class have had in that country. In the larger towns it forms almost the majority of the inhabitants; in the smaller ones it entirely predominates, from the absence of wealthier competitors or influence. This class, a most important one in every body politic, and in all modern revolutions, is still more important in Germany, where, during the recent struggles, it generally played the decisive part. Its intermediate position between the class of larger capitalists, traders, and manufacturers, the bourgeoisie properly so-called, and the proletarian or industrial class, determines its character.

Aspiring to the position of the first, the least adverse turn of fortune hurls the individuals of this class down into the ranks of the second. In monarchical and feudal countries the custom of the court and aristocracy becomes necessary to its existence; the loss of this custom might ruin a great part of it. In the smaller towns a military garrison, a county government, a court of law with its followers, form very often the base of its prosperity; withdraw these, and down go the shopkeepers, the tailors, the shoemakers, the joiners. Thus eternally tossed about between the hope of entering the ranks of the wealthier class, and the fear of being reduced to the state of proletarians or even paupers; between the hope of promoting their interests by conquering a share in the direction of public affairs, and the dread of rousing, by ill-timed opposition, the ire of a Government which disposes of their very existence, because it has the power of removing their best customers; possessed of small means, the insecurity of the possession of which is in the inverse ratio of the amount,—this class is extremely vacillating in its views. Humble and crouchingly submissive under a powerful feudal or monarchical Government, it turns to the side of Liberalism when the middle class is in the ascendant; it becomes seized with violent democratic fits as soon as the middle class has secured its own supremacy, but falls back into the abject despondency of fear as soon as the class below itself, the proletarians, attempts an independent movement. We shall by and by see this class, in Germany, pass alternately from one of these stages to the other.

The working class in Germany is, in its social and political development, as far behind that of England and France as the German bourgeoisie is behind the bourgeoisie of those countries. Like master, like man. The evolution of the conditions of existence for a numerous, strong, concentrated, and intelligent proletarian class goes hand in hand with the development of the conditions of existence for a numerous, wealthy, concentrated, and powerful middle class. The working-class movement itself never is independent, never is of an exclusively proletarian character until all the different factions of the middle class, and particularly its most progressive faction, the large manufacturers, have conquered political power, and remodelled the State according to their wants. It is then that the inevitable conflict between the employer and the employed becomes imminent, and cannot be adjourned any longer; that the working class can no longer be put off with delusive hopes and promises never to be realised; that the great problem of the nineteenth century, the abolition of the proletariat, is at last brought forward fairly and in its proper light. Now, in Germany the mass of the working class were employed, not by those modern manufacturing lords of which Great Britain furnishes such splendid specimens, but by small tradesmen, whose entire manufacturing system is a mere relic of the Middle Ages. And as there is an enormous difference between the great cotton lord and the petty cobbler or master tailor, so there is a corresponding distance from the wide-awake factory operative of modern manufacturing Babylons to the bashful journeyman tailor or cabinet-maker of a small country town, who lives in circumstances and works after a plan very little different from those of the like sort of men some five hundred years ago. This general absence of modern conditions of life, of modern modes of industrial production, of course, was accompanied by a pretty equally general absence of modern ideas, and it is, therefore, not to be wondered at if, at the outbreak of the Revolution, a large part of the working classes should cry out for the immediate re-establishment of guilds and Mediæval privileged trades corporations. Yet from the manufacturing districts, where the modern system of production predominated, and in consequence of the facilities of intercommunication and mental development afforded by the migratory life of a large number of the working men, a strong nucleus formed itself, whose ideas about the emancipation of their class were far clearer and more in accordance with existing facts and historical necessities; but they were a mere minority. If the active movement of the middle classes may be dated from 1840, that of the working class commences its advent by the insurrections of the Silesian and Bohemian factory operatives in 1844, and we shall soon have occasion to pass in review the different stages through which this movement passed.

Lastly, there was the great class of the small farmers, the peasantry, which, with its appendix of farm labourers, constitutes a considerable majority of the entire nation. But this class again subdivided itself into different fractions. There were, firstly, the more wealthy farmers, what is called in Germany *Gross* and *Mittel-Bauern*, proprietors of more or less extensive

B

farms, and each of them commanding the services of several agricultural labourers. This class, placed between the large untaxed feudal landowners, and the smaller peasantry and farm labourers, for obvious reasons found in an alliance with the anti-feudal middle class of the towns its most natural political course. Then there were, secondly, the small freeholders, predominating in the Rhine country, where feudalism had succumbed before the mighty strokes of the great French Revolution. Similar independent small freeholders also existed here and there in other provinces, where they had succeeded in buying off the feudal charges formerly due upon their lands. This class, however, was a class of freeholders by name only, their property being generally mortgaged to such an extent, and under such onerous conditions, that not the peasant, but the usurer who had advanced the money, was the real landowner. Thirdly, the feudal tenants, who could not be easily turned out of their holdings, but who had to pay a perpetual rent, or to perform in perpetuity a certain amount of labour in favour of the lord of the manor. Lastly, the agricultural labourers, whose condition, in many large farming concerns, was exactly that of the same class in England, and who in all cases lived and died poor, ill-fed, and the slaves of their employers. These three latter classes of the agricultural population, the small freeholders, the feudal tenants, and the agricultural labourers, never troubled their heads much about politics before the Revolution, but it is evident that this event must have opened to them a new career, full of brilliant prospects. To every one of them the Revolution offered advantages, and the movement once fairly engaged in, it was to be expected that each, in their turn, would join it. But at the same time it is quite as evident, and equally borne out by the history of all modern countries, that the agricultural population, in consequence of its dispersion over a great space, and of the difficulty of bringing about an agreement among any considerable portion of it, never can attempt a successful independent movement; they require the initiatory impulse of the more concentrated, more enlightened, more easily moved people of the towns.

The preceding short sketch of the most important of the classes, which in their aggregate formed the German nation at the outbreak of the recent movements, will already be sufficient to explain a great part of the incoherence, incongruence, and apparent contradiction which prevailed in that movement. When interests so varied, so conflicting, so strangely crossing each other, are brought into violent collision; when these contending interests in every district, every province, are mixed in different proportions; when, above all, there is no great centre in the country, no London, no Paris, the decisions of which, by their weight, may supersede the necessity of fighting out the same quarrel over and over again in every single locality; what else is to be expected but that the contest will dissolve itself into a mass of unconnected struggles, in which an enormous quantity of blood, energy, and capital is spent, but which for all that remain without any decisive results?

The political dismemberment of Germany into three dozen of more or less important principalities is equally explained by this confusion and multiplicity of the elements which compose the nation, and which again vary in every locality. Where there are no common interests there can be no unity of purpose, much less of action. The German Confederation, it is true, was declared everlastingly indissoluble; yet the Confederation, and its organ, the Diet, never represented German unity. The very highest pitch to which centralisation was ever carried in Germany was the establishment of the Zollverein; by this the States on the North Sea were also forced into a Customs Union of their own, Austria remaining wrapped up in her separate prohibitive tariff. Germany had the satisfaction to be, for all practical purposes, divided between three independent powers only, instead of between thirty-six. Of course the paramount supremacy of the Russian Czar, as established in 1814, underwent no change on this account.

Having drawn these preliminary conclusions from our premisses, we shall see, in our next, how the aforesaid various classes of the German people were set into movement one after the other, and what character the movement assumed on the outbreak of the French Revolution of 1848.

New York Daily Tribune, October 25th, 1851.

II

London, September 1851.

THE political movement of the middle class or bourgeoisie, in Germany, may be dated from 1840. It had been preceded by symptoms showing that the moneyed and industrial class of that country was ripening into a state which would no longer allow it to continue apathetic and passive under the pressure of a half-feudal, half-bureaucratic Monarchism. The smaller princes of Germany, partly to insure to themselves a greater independence against the supremacy of Austria and Prussia, or against the influence of the nobility of their own States, partly in order to consolidate into a whole the disconnected provinces united under their rule by the Congress of Vienna, one after the other granted constitutions of a more or less liberal character. They could do so without any danger to themselves; for if the Diet of the Confederation, this mere puppet of Austria and Prussia, was to encroach upon their independence as sovereigns, they knew that in resisting its dictates they would be backed by public opinion and the Chambers; and if, on the contrary, these Chambers grew too strong, they could readily command the power of the Diet to break down all opposition. The Bavarian, Würtemberg, Baden or Hanoverian Constitutional institutions could not, under such circumstances, give rise to any serious struggle for political power, and, therefore, the great bulk of the German middle class kept very generally aloof from the petty squabbles raised in the Legislatures of the small States, well knowing that without a fundamental change in the policy and constitution of the two great powers of Germany, no secondary efforts and victories would be of any avail. But, at the same time, a race of Liberal lawyers, professional oppositionists, sprung up in these small assemblies: the Rottecks, the Welckers, the Roemers, the Jordans, the Stüves, the Eisenmanns, those great "popular men" (*Volksmänner*) who, after a more or less noisy, but always unsuccessful, opposition of twenty years, were carried to the summit of power by the revolutionary springtide of 1848, and who, after having there shown their utter impotency and insignificance, were hurled down again in a moment. These first specimens upon German soil of the trader in politics and opposition, by their speeches and writings made familiar to the German ear the language of Constitutionalism, and by their very existence foreboded the approach of a time when the middle class would seize upon and restore to their proper meaning political phrases which these talkative attorneys and professors were in the habit of using without knowing much about the sense originally attached to them.

German literature, too, laboured under the influence of the political excitement into which all Europe had been thrown by the events of 1830. A crude Constitutionalism, or a still cruder Republicanism, were preached by almost all writers of the time. It became more and more the habit, particularly of the inferior sorts of literati, to make up for the want of cleverness in their productions, by political allusions which were sure to attract attention. Poetry, novels, reviews, the drama, every literary production teemed with what was called " tendency," that is with more or less timid exhibitions of an anti-governmental spirit. In order to complete the confusion of ideas reigning after 1830 in Germany, with these elements of political opposition there were mixed up ill-digested university-recollections of German philosophy, and misunderstood gleanings from French Socialism, particularly Saint-Simonism; and the clique of writers who expatiated upon this heterogeneous conglomerate of ideas, presumptuously called themselves " Young Germany," or " the Modern School." They have since repented their youthful sins, but not improved their style of writing.

Lastly, German philosophy, that most complicated, but at the same time most sure, thermometer of the development of the German mind, had declared for the middle class, when Hegel in his *Philosophy of Law* pronounced Constitutional Monarchy to be the final and most perfect form of government. In other words, he proclaimed the approaching advent of the middle classes of the country to political power. His school, after his death, did not stop here. While the more advanced section of his followers, on one hand, subjected every religious belief to the ordeal of a rigorous criticism, and shook to its foundation the ancient fabric of Christianity, they at the same time brought forward bolder political principles than hitherto it had been the fate of German ears to hear expounded, and attempted to restore to glory the memory of the heroes of the first French Revolution. The abstruse philosophical language in which these ideas were clothed, if it obscured the mind of both the writer and the reader, equally blinded the eyes of the censor, and thus it was that the " young Hegelian " writers enjoyed a liberty of the Press unknown in every other branch of literature.

Thus it was evident that public opinion was undergoing a great change in Germany. By degrees the vast majority of those classes whose education or position in life enabled them, under an Absolute Monarchy, to gain some political information, and to form anything like an independent political opinion, united into one mighty phalanx of opposition against the existing system. And in passing judgment upon the slowness of political development in Germany no one ought to omit taking into account the difficulty of obtaining correct information upon any subject in a country where all sources of information were under the control of the Government, where from the Ragged School and the Sunday School to the Newspaper and University nothing was said, taught, printed, or published but what had previously obtained its approbation. Look at Vienna, for instance. The people of Vienna, in industry and manufactures, second to none perhaps in Germany; in spirit, courage, and revolutionary energy, proving themselves far superior to all, were yet more ignorant as to their real interests, and committed more blunders during the Revolution than any others, and this was due in a very great measure to the almost absolute ignorance with regard to the very commonest political subjects in which Metternich's Government had succeeded in keeping them.

It needs no further explanation why, under such a system, political information was an almost exclusive monopoly of such classes of society as could afford to pay for its being smuggled into the country, and more particularly of those whose interests were most seriously attacked by the existing state of things, namely, the manufacturing and commercial classes. They, therefore, were the first to unite in a mass against the continuance of a more or less disguised Absolutism, and from their passing into the ranks of the opposition must be dated the beginning of the real revolutionary movement in Germany.

The oppositional pronunciamento of the German bourgeoisie may be dated from 1840, from the death of the late King of Prussia, the last surviving founder of the Holy Alliance of 1815. The new King was known to be no supporter of the predominantly bureaucratic and military monarchy of his father. What the French middle class had expected from the advent of Louis XVI, the German bourgeoisie hoped, in some measure, from Frederick William IV of Prussia. It was agreed upon all hands that the old system was exploded, worn out, and must be given up; and what had been borne in silence under the old King now was loudly proclaimed to be intolerable.

But if Louis XVI, " Louis le Désiré," had been a plain, unpretending simpleton, half conscious of his own nullity, without any fixed opinions, ruled principally by the habits contracted during his education, " Frederick William le Désiré " was something quite different. While he certainly surpassed his French original in weakness of character, he was neither without pretensions nor without opinions. He had made himself acquainted, in an amateur sort of way, with the rudiments of most sciences, and thought himself, therefore, learned enough to consider final his judgment upon every subject. He made sure he was a first-rate orator, and there was certainly no commercial traveller in Berlin who could beat him either in prolixity of pretended wit, or in fluency of elocution. And, above all, he had his opinions. He hated and despised the bureaucratic element of the Prussian Monarchy, but only because all his sympathies were with the feudal element. Himself one of the founders of, and chief contributors to, the *Berlin Political Weekly Paper*, the so-called Historical School (a school living upon the ideas of Bonald, De Maistre, and other writers of the first generation of French Legitimists), he aimed at a restoration, as complete as possible, of the predominant social position of the nobility. The King, first nobleman of his realm, surrounded in the first instance by a splendid court of mighty vassals, princes, dukes, and counts; in the second instance, by a numerous and wealthy lower nobility; ruling according to his discretion over his loyal burgesses and peasants, and thus being himself the chief of a complete hierarchy of social ranks or castes, each of which was to enjoy its particular privileges, and to be separated from the others by the almost insurmountable barrier of birth, or of a fixed, inalterable social position; the whole of these castes, or " estates of the realm " balancing each other at the same time so nicely in power and influence that a complete independence of action should remain to the King—such was the beau-ideal which Frederick William IV undertook to realise, and which he is again trying to realise at the present moment.

It took some time before the Prussian bourgeoisie, not very well versed in theoretical questions, found out the real purport of their King's tendency. But what they very soon found out was the fact that he was bent upon things quite the reverse of what they wanted. Hardly did the new King find his " gift of the gab " unfettered by his father's death than he set about proclaiming his intentions in speeches without number; and every speech, every act of his, went far to estrange from him the sympathies of the middle class. He would not have cared much for that, if it had not been for some stern and startling realities which interrupted his poetic dreams. Alas, that romanticism is not very quick at accounts, and that feudalism, ever since Don Quixote, reckons without its host! Frederick William IV partook too much of that contempt of ready cash which ever has been the noblest inheritance of the sons of the Crusaders. He found at his accession a costly, although parsimoniously arranged system of government, and a moderately filled State Treasury. In two years every trace of a surplus was spent in court festivals, royal progresses, largesses, subventions to needy, seedy, and greedy noblemen, etc., and the regular taxes were no longer sufficient for the exigencies of either Court or Government. And thus His Majesty found himself very soon placed between a glaring deficit on one side, and a law of 1820 on the other, by which any new loan, or any increase of the then existing taxation was made illegal without the assent of " the future Representation of the People." This representation did not exist; the new King was less inclined than even his father to create it; and if he had been, he knew that public opinion had wonderfully changed since his accession.

Indeed, the middle classes, who had partly expected that the new King would at once grant a Constitution, proclaim the Liberty of the Press, Trial by Jury, etc., etc.—in short, himself take the lead of that peaceful revolution which they wanted in order to obtain political supremacy—the middle classes had found out their error, and had turned ferociously against the King. In the Rhine Provinces, and more or less generally all over Prussia, they were so exasperated that they, being short themselves of men able to represent them in the Press, went to the length of an alliance with the extreme philosophical party, of which we have spoken above. The fruit of this alliance was the *Rhenish Gazette* of Cologne, a paper which was suppressed after fifteen months' existence, but from which may be dated the existence of the Newspaper Press in Germany. This was in 1842.

The poor King, whose commercial difficulties were the keenest satire upon his Mediæval propensities, very soon found out that he could not continue to reign without making some slight concession to the popular outcry for that " Representation of the People," which, as the last remnant of the long-forgotten promises of 1813 and 1815, had been embodied in the law of 1820. He found the least objectionable mode of satisfying this untoward law in calling together the Standing Committees of the Provincial Diets. The Provincial Diets had been instituted in 1823. They consisted for every one of the eight provinces of the kingdom: (1) Of the higher nobility, the formerly sovereign families of the German Empire, the heads of which were members of the Diet by birthright. (2) Of the representatives of the knights, or lower nobility. (3) Of representatives of towns. (4) Of deputies of the peasantry, or small farming class. The whole was arranged in such a manner that in every province the two sections of the nobility always had a majority of the Diet. Every one of these eight Provincial Diets elected a Committee, and these eight Committees were now called to Berlin in order to form a Representative Assembly for the purpose of voting the much-desired loan. It was stated that the Treasury was full, and that the loan was required, not for current wants, but for the construction of a State railway. But the united Committees gave the King a flat refusal, declaring themselves incompetent to act as the representatives of the people, and called upon His Majesty to fulfil the promise of a Representative Constitution which his father had given, when he wanted the aid of the people against Napoleon.

The sitting of the united Committees proved that the spirit of opposition was no longer confined to the bourgeoisie. A part of the peasantry had joined them, and many nobles, being themselves large farmers on their own properties, and dealers in corn, wool, spirits, and flax, requiring the same guarantees against absolutism, bureaucracy, and feudal restoration, had equally pronounced against the Government, and for a Representative Constitution. The King's plan had signally failed; he had got no money, and had increased the power of the opposition. The subsequent sitting of the Provincial Diets themselves was still more unfortunate for the King. All of them asked for reforms, for the fulfilment of the promises of 1813 and 1815, for a Constitution and a Free Press; the resolutions to this effect of some of them were rather disrespectfully worded, and the ill-humoured replies of the exasperated King made the evil still greater.

In the meantime, the financial difficulties of the Government went on increasing. For a time, abatements made upon the moneys appropriated for the different public services, fraudulent transactions with the "Seehandlung," a commercial establishment speculating and trading for account and risk of the State, and long since acting as its money-broker, had sufficed to keep up appearances; increased issues of State paper-money had furnished some resources; and the secret, upon the whole, had been pretty well kept. But all these contrivances were soon exhausted. There was another plan tried: the establishment of a bank, the capital of which was to be furnished partly by the State and partly by private shareholders; the chief direction to belong to the State, in such a manner as to enable the Government to draw upon the funds of this bank to a large amount, and thus to repeat the same fraudulent transactions that would no longer do with the "Seehandlung." But, as a matter of course, there were no capitalists to be found who would hand over their money upon such conditions; the statutes of the bank had to be altered, and the property of the shareholders guaranteed from the encroachments of the Treasury, before any shares were subscribed for. Thus, this plan having failed, there remained nothing but to try a loan, if capitalists could be found who would lend their cash without requiring the permission and guarantee of that mysterious "future Representation of the People." Rothschild was applied to, and he declared that if the loan was to be guaranteed by this "Representation of the People," he would undertake the thing at a moment's notice—if not, he could not have anything to do with the transaction.

Thus every hope of obtaining money had vanished, and there was no possibility of escaping the fatal " Representation of the People." Rothschild's refusal was known in autumn, 1846, and in February of the next year the King called together all the eight Provincial Diets to Berlin, forming them into one " United Diet." This Diet was to do the work required, in case of need, by the law of 1820; it was to vote loans and increase taxes, but beyond that it was to have no rights. Its voice upon general legislation was to be merely consultative; it was to assemble, not at fixed periods, but whenever it pleased the King; it was to discuss nothing but what the Government pleased to lay before it. Of course, the members were very little satisfied with the part they were expected to perform. They repeated the wishes they had enounced when they met in the provincial assemblies; the relations between them and the Government soon became acrimonious, and when the loan, which was again stated to be required for railway construction, was demanded from them, they again refused to grant it.

This vote very soon brought their sitting to a close. The King, more and more exasperated, dismissed them with a reprimand, but still remained without money. And, indeed, he had every reason to be alarmed at his position, seeing that the Liberal League, headed by the middle classes, comprising a large part of the lower nobility, and all the manifold discontents that had been accumulated in the different sections of the lower orders—that this Liberal League was determined to have what it wanted. In vain the King had declared, in the opening speech, that he would never, never grant a Constitution in the modern sense of the word; the Liberal League insisted upon such a modern, anti-feudal, Representative Constitution, with all its sequels, Liberty of the Press, Trial by Jury, etc.; and before they got it, not a farthing of money would they grant. There was one thing evident: that things could not go on long in this manner, and that either one of the parties must give way, or that a rupture—a bloody struggle—must ensue. And the middle classes knew that they were on the eve of a revolution, and they prepared themselves for it. They sought to obtain by every possible means the support of the working class of the towns, and of the peasantry in the agricultural districts, and it is well known that there was, in the latter end of 1847, hardly a single prominent political character among the bourgeoisie who did not proclaim himself a " Socialist," in order to insure to himself the sympathy of the proletarian class. We shall see these " Socialists " at work by and by.

This eagerness of the leading bourgeoisie to adopt, at least, the outward show of Socialism, was caused by a great change that had come over the working classes of Germany. There had been ever since 1840 a fraction of German workmen, who, travelling in France and Switzerland, had more or less imbibed the crude Socialist or Communist notions then current among the French workmen. The increasing attention paid to similar ideas in France ever since 1840 made Socialism and Communism fashionable in Germany also, and as far back as 1843, all newspapers teemed with discussions of social questions. A school of Socialists very soon formed itself in Germany, distinguished more for the obscurity than for the novelty of its ideas; its principal efforts consisted in the translation of French Fourierist, Saint-Simonian, and other doctrines into the abstruse language of German philosophy. The German Communist school, entirely different from this sect, was formed about the same time.

In 1844, there occurred the Silesian weavers' riots, followed by the insurrection of the calico printers of Prague. These riots, cruelly suppressed, riots of working men not against the Government, but against their employers, created a deep sensation, and gave a new stimulus to Socialist and Communist propaganda amongst the working people. So did the bread riots during the year of famine, 1847. In short, in the same manner as Constitutional Opposition rallied around its banner the great bulk of the propertied classes (with the exception of the large feudal land-holders), so the working classes of the larger towns looked for their emancipation to the Socialist and Communist doctrines, although, under the then existing Press laws, they could be made to know only very little about them. They could not be expected to have any very definite ideas as to what they wanted; they only knew that the programme of the Constitutional bourgeoisie did not contain all they wanted, and that their wants were no wise contained in the Constitutional circle of ideas.

There was then no separate Republican party in Germany.

People were either Constitutional Monarchists, or more or less clearly defined Socialists or Communists.

With such elements the lightest collision must have brought about a great revolution. While the higher nobility and the older civil and military officers were the only safe supports of the existing system; while the lower nobility, the trading middle classes, the universities, the schoolmasters of every degree, and even part of the lower ranks of the bureaucracy and military officers were all leagued against the Government; while behind these there stood the dissatisfied masses of the peasantry, and of the proletarians of the large towns, supporting, for the time being, the Liberal Opposition, but already muttering strange words about taking things into their own hands; while the bourgeoisie was ready to hurl down the Government, and the proletarians were preparing to hurl down the bourgeoisie in its turn; this Government went on obstinately in a course which must bring about a collision. Germany was, in the beginning of 1848, on the eve of a revolution, and this revolution was sure to come, even had the French Revolution of February not hastened it.

What the effects of this Parisian Revolution were upon Germany we shall see in our next.

New York Daily Tribune, October 28th, 1851.

III

London, September 1851.

In our last we confined ourselves almost exclusively to that State which, during the years 1840 to 1848, was by far the most important in the German movement, namely, to Prussia. It is, however, time to pass a rapid glance over the other States of Germany during the same period.

As to the petty States, they had, ever since the revolutionary movements of 1830, completely passed under the dictatorship of the Diet, that is of Austria and Prussia. The several Constitutions, established as much as a means of defence against the dictates of the larger States, as to insure popularity to their princely authors, and unity to heterogeneous Assemblies of Provinces, formed by the Congress of Vienna, without any leading principle whatever—these Constitutions, illusory as they were, had yet proved dangerous to the authority of the petty princes themselves during the exciting times of 1830 and 1831. They were all but destroyed; whatever of them was allowed to remain was less than a shadow, and it required the loquacious self-complacency of a Welcker, a Rotteck, a Dahlmann, to imagine that any results could possibly flow from the humble opposition, mingled with degrading flattery, which they were allowed to show off in the impotent Chambers of these petty States.

The more energetic portion of the middle class in these smaller States, very soon after 1840, abandoned all the hopes they had formerly based upon the development of Parliamentary government in these dependencies of Austria and Prussia. No sooner had the Prussian bourgeoisie and the classes allied to it shown a serious resolution to struggle for Parliamentary government in Prussia, than they were allowed to take the lead of the Constitutional movement over all non-Austrian Germany. It is a fact which now will not any longer be contested, that the nucleus of those Constitutionalists of Central Germany, who afterwards seceded from the Frankfort National Assembly, and who, from the place of their separate meetings, were called the Gotha party, long before 1848 contemplated a plan which, with little modification, they in 1849 proposed to the representatives of all Germany. They intended a complete exclusion of Austria from the German Confederation, the establishment of a new Confederation, with a new fundamental law, and with a Federal Parliament, under the protection of Prussia, and the incorporation of the more insignificant States into the larger ones. All this was to be carried out the moment Prussia entered into the ranks of Constitutional Monarchy, established the Liberty of the Press, assumed a policy independent from that of Russia and Austria, and thus enabled the Constitutionalists of the lesser States to obtain a real control over their respective Governments. The inventor of this scheme was Professor Gervinus, of Heidelberg (Baden). Thus the emancipation of the Prussian bourgeoisie was to be the signal for that of the middle classes of Germany generally, and for an alliance, offensive and defensive, of both against Russia and Austria, for Austria was, as we shall see presently, considered as an entirely barbarian country, of which very little was known, and that little not to the credit of its population; Austria, therefore, was not considered as an essential part of Germany.

As to the other classes of society, in the smaller States they followed, more or less rapidly, in the wake of their equals in Prussia. The shopkeeping class got more and more dissatisfied with their respective Governments, with the increase of taxation, with the curtailments of those political sham-privileges of which they used to boast when comparing themselves to the " slaves of despotism " in Austria and Prussia; but as yet they had nothing definite in their opposition which might stamp them as an independent party, distinct from the Constitutionalism of the higher bourgeoisie. The dissatisfaction among the peasantry was equally growing, but it is well known that this section of the people, in quiet and peaceful times, will never assert its interests and assume its position as an independent class, except in countries where universal suffrage is established. The working classes in the trades and manufactures of the towns commenced to be infected with the " poison " of Socialism and Communism, but there being few towns of any importance out of Prussia, and still fewer manufacturing districts, the movement of this class, owing to the want of centres of action and propaganda, was extremely slow in the smaller States.

Both in Prussia and in the smaller States the difficulty of giving vent to political opposition created a sort of religious opposition in the parallel movements of German Catholicism and Free Congregationalism. History affords us numerous examples where, in countries which enjoy the blessings of a State Church, and where political discussion is fettered, the profane and dangerous opposition against the worldly power is hid under the more sanctified and apparently more disinterested struggle against spiritual despotism. Many a Government that will not allow of any of its acts being discussed, will hestitate before it creates martyrs and excites the religious fanaticism of the masses. Thus in Germany, in 1845, in every State, either the Roman Catholic or the Protestant religion, or both, were considered part and parcel of the law of the land. In every State, too, the clergy of either of those denominations, or of both, formed an essential part of the bureaucratic establishment of the Government. To attack Protestant or Catholic orthodoxy, to attack priestcraft, was then to make an underhand attack upon the Government itself. As to the German Catholics, their very existence was an attack upon the Catholic Governments of Germany, particularly Austria and Bavaria; and as such it was taken by those Governments. The Free Congregationalists, Protestant Dissenters, somewhat resembling the English and American Unitarians, openly professed their opposition to the clerical and rigidly orthodox tendency of the King of Prussia and his favourite Minister for the Educational and Clerical Department, Mr. Eickhorn. The two new sects, rapidly extending for a moment, the first in Catholic, the second in Protestant countries, had no other distinction but their different origin; as to their tenets, they perfectly agreed upon this most important point—that all definite dogmas were nugatory. This want of any definition was their very essence; they pretended to build that great temple under the roof of which all Germans might unite; they thus represented, in a religious form, another political idea of the day—that of German unity, and yet they could never agree among themselves.

The idea of German unity, which the above-mentioned sects

sought to realise, at least, upon religious ground, by inventing a common religion for all Germans, manufactured expressly for their use, habits, and taste—this idea was, indeed, very widely spread, particularly in the smaller States. Ever since the dissolution of the German Empire by Napoleon, the cry for a union of all the *disjecta membra* of the German body had been the most general expression of discontent with the established order of things, and most so in the smaller States, where the costliness of a court, an administration, an army, in short, the dead weight of taxation, increased in a direct ratio with the smallness and impotency of the State. But what this German unity was to be when carried out was a question upon which parties disagreed. The bourgeoisie, which wanted no serious revolutionary convulsions, were satisfied with what we have seen they considered "practicable," namely, a union of all Germany, exclusive of Austria, under the supremacy of a Constitutional Government of Prussia; and surely, without conjuring dangerous storms, nothing more could, at that time, be done. The shopkeeping class and the peasantry, as far as these latter troubled themselves about such things, never arrived at any definition of that German unity they so loudly clamoured after; a few dreamers, mostly feudalist reactionists, hoped for the re-establishment of the German Empire; some few ignorant, soi-disant Radicals, admiring Swiss institutions, of which they had not yet made that practical experience which afterwards most ludicrously undeceived them, pronounced for a Federated Republic; and it was only the most extreme party which, at that time, dared pronounce for a German Republic, one and indivisible. Thus, German unity was in itself a question big with disunion, discord, and, in the case of certain eventualities, even civil war.

To resume, then; this was the state of Prussia, and the smaller States of Germany, at the end of 1847. The middle class, feeling their power, and resolved not to endure much longer the fetters with which a feudal and bureaucratic despotism enchained their commercial transactions, their industrial productivity, their common action as a class; a portion of the landed nobility so far changed into producers of mere marketable commodities, as to have the same interests and to make common cause with the middle class; the smaller trading class, dissatisfied, grumbling at the taxes, at the impediments thrown in the way of their business, but without any definite plan for such reforms as should secure their position in the social and political body; the peasantry, oppressed here by feudal exactions, there by money-lenders, usurers, and lawyers; the working people of the towns infected with the general discontent, equally hating the Government and the large industrial capitalists, and catching the contagion of Socialist and Communist ideas; in short, a heterogeneous mass of opposition, springing from various interests, but more or less led on by the bourgeoisie, in the first ranks of which again marched the bourgeoisie of Prussia, and particularly of the Rhine Province. On the other hand, Governments disagreeing upon many points, distrustful of each other, and particularly of that of Prussia, upon which yet they had to rely for protection; in Prussia a Government forsaken by public opinion, forsaken by even a portion of the nobility, leaning upon an army and a bureaucracy which every day got more infected by the ideas, and subjected to the influence, of the oppositional bourgeoisie— a Government, besides all this, penniless in the most literal meaning of the word, and which could not procure a single cent to cover its increasing deficit, but by surrendering at discretion to the opposition of the bourgeoisie. Was there ever a more splendid position for the middle class of any country, while it struggled for power against the established Government?

New York Daily Tribune, November 6th, 1851.

IV

London, September 1851.

We have now to consider Austria; that country which, up to March 1848, was sealed up to the eyes of foreign nations almost as much as China before the late war with England.

As a matter of course, we can here take into consideration nothing but German Austria. The affairs of the Polish, Hungarian, or Italian Austrians do not belong to our subject, and as far as they, since 1848, have influenced the fate of the German Austrians, they will have to be taken into account hereafter.

The Government of Prince Metternich turned upon two hinges; firstly, to keep every one of the different nations subjected to the Austrian rule, in check, by all other nations similarly conditioned; secondly, and this always has been the fundamental principle of absolute monarchies, to rely for support upon two classes, the feudal landlords and the large stock-jobbing capitalists; and to balance, at the same time, the influence and power of either of these classes by that of the other, so as to leave full independence of action to the Government. The landed nobility, whose entire income consisted in feudal revenues of all sorts, could not but support a Government which proved their only protection against that downtrodden class of serfs upon whose spoils they lived; and whenever the less wealthy portion of them, as in Galicia, in 1846, rose in opposition against the Government, Metternich in an instant let loose upon them these very serfs, who at any rate profited by the occasion to wreak a terrible vengeance upon their more immediate oppressors. On the other hand, the large capitalists of the Exchange were chained to Metternich's Government by the vast share they had in the public funds of the country. Austria, restored to her full power in 1815, restoring, and maintaining in Italy Absolute Monarchy ever since 1820, freed from part of her liabilities by the bankruptcy of 1810, had, after the peace, very soon re-established her credit in the great European money markets; and in proportion as her credit grew, she had drawn against it. Thus all the large European money-dealers had engaged considerable portions of their capital in the Austrian funds; they all of them were interested in upholding the credit of that country, and as Austrian public credit, in order to be upheld, ever required new loans, they were obliged from time to time to advance new capital in order to keep up the credit of the securities for that which they already had advanced. The long peace after 1815, and the apparent impossibility of a thousand years' old empire, like Austria, being upset, increased the credit of Metternich's Government in a wonderful ratio, and made it even independent of the goodwill of the Vienna bankers and stock-jobbers; for as long as Metternich could obtain plenty of money at Frankfort and Amsterdam, he had, of course, the satisfaction of seeing the Austrian capitalists at his feet. They were, besides, in every other respect at his mercy; the large profits which bankers, stock-jobbers, and Government contractors always contrive to draw out of an absolute monarchy, were compensated for by the almost unlimited power which the Government possessed over their persons and fortunes; and not the smallest shadow of an opposition was, therefore, to be expected from this quarter. Thus Metternich was sure of the support of the two most powerful and influential classes of the empire, and he possessed besides an army and a bureaucracy, which for all purposes of absolutism could not be better constituted. The civil and military officers in the Austrian service form a race of their own; their fathers have been in the service of the Kaiser, and so will their sons be; they belong to none of the multifarious nationalities congregated under the wing of the double-headed eagle; they are, and ever have been, removed from one end of the empire to the other, from Poland to Italy, from Germany to Transylvania; Hungarian, Pole, German, Roumanian, Italian, Croat, every individual not stamped with "imperial and royal authority," etc., bearing a separate national character, is equally despised by them; they have no nationality, or rather, they alone make up the really Austrian nation. It is evident what a pliable, and at the same time powerful instrument, in the hands of an intelligent and energetic chief, such a civil and military hierarchy must be.

As to the other classes of the population, Metternich, in the true spirit of a statesman of the *ancien régime*, cared little for their support. He had, with regard to them, but one policy: to draw as much as possible out of them in the shape of taxation, and at the same time to keep them quiet. The trading and manufacturing middle class was but of slow growth in Austria. The trade of the Danube was comparatively unimportant; the country possessed but one port, Trieste, and the trade of the port was very limited. As to the manufacturers, they enjoyed considerable protection, amounting even in most cases to the complete exclusion of all foreign competition; but this advantage had been granted to them principally with a view to increase their tax-paying capabilities, and was in a high degree counterpoised by internal restrictions on manufactures, privileges on guilds, and other feudal corporations, which were scrupulously upheld as long as they did not impede the purposes and views of the Government. The petty tradesmen were encased in the narrow bounds of these Mediæval guilds, which kept the different trades in a perpetual war of privilege against each other, and at the same time, by all but excluding individuals of the working class from the possibility of raising themselves in the social scale, gave a sort of hereditary stability to the members of those involuntary associations. Lastly, the peasant and the working man were treated as mere taxable matter, and the only care that was taken of them was to keep them as much as possible in the same conditions of life in which they then existed, and in which their fathers had existed before them. For this purpose every old, established, hereditary authority was upheld in the same manner as that of the State; the authority of the landlord over the petty tenant farmer, that of the manufacturer over the operative, of the small master over the journeyman and apprentice, of the father over the son, was everywhere rigidly maintained by the Government, and every branch of disobedience punished the same as a transgression of the law, by that universal instrument of Austrian justice—the stick.

Finally, to wind up into one comprehensive system all these attempts at creating an artificial stability, the intellectual food allowed to the nation was selected with the minutest caution, and dealt out as sparingly as possible. Education was everywhere in the hands of the Catholic priesthood, whose chiefs, in the same manner as the large feudal landowners, were deeply interested in the conservation of the existing system. The universities were organised in a manner which allowed them to produce nothing but special men, that might or might not obtain great proficiency in sundry particular branches of knowledge, but which, at all events, excluded that universal liberal education which other universities are expected to impart. There was absolutely no newspaper press, except in Hungary, and the Hungarian papers were prohibited in all other parts of the monarchy. As to general literature, its range had not widened for a century; it had narrowed again after the death of Joseph II. And all around the frontier, wherever the Austrian States touched upon a civilised country, a cordon of literary censors was established in connection with the cordon of customhouse officials, preventing any foreign book or newspaper from passing into Austria before its contents had been twice or three times thoroughly sifted, and found pure of even the slightest contamination of the malignant spirit of the age.

For about thirty years after 1815 this system worked with wonderful success. Austria remained almost unknown to Europe, and Europe was quite as little known in Austria. The social state of every class of the population, and of the population as a whole, appeared not to have undergone the slightest change. Whatever rancour there might exist from class to class—and the existence of this rancour was for Metternich a principal condition of government, which he even fostered by making the higher classes the instruments of all Government exactions, and thus throwing the odium upon them—whatever hatred the people might bear to the inferior officials of the State, there existed, upon the whole, little or no dissatisfaction with the Central Government. The Emperor was adored, and old Francis I seemed to be borne out by facts when, doubting of the durability of this system, he complacently added: " And yet it will hold while I live, and Metternich."

But there was a slow underground movement going on which baffled all Metternich's efforts. The wealth and influence of the manufacturing and trading middle class increased. The introduction of machinery and steam-power in manufactures upset in Austria, as it had done everywhere else, the old relations and vital conditions of whole classes of society; it changed serfs into free men, small farmers into manufacturing operatives; it undermined the old feudal trades corporations, and destroyed the means of existence of many of them. The new commercial and manufacturing population came everywhere into collision with the old feudal institutions. The middle classes, more and more induced by their business to travel abroad, introduced some mythical knowledge of the civilised countries situated beyond the Imperial line of customs; the introduction of railways finally accelerated both the industrial and intellectual movement. There was, too, a dangerous part in the Austrian State establishment, viz., the Hungarian feudal Constitution, with its parliamentary proceedings, and its struggles of the impoverished and oppositional mass of the nobility against the Government and its allies, the magnates. Presburg, the seat of the Diet, was at the very gates of Vienna. All the elements contributed to create among the middle classes of the towns a spirit, not exactly of opposition, for opposition was as yet impossible, but of discontent; a general wish for reforms, more of an administrative than of a constitutional nature. And in the same manner as in Prussia, a portion of the bureaucracy joined the bourgeoisie. Among this hereditary caste of officials the traditions of Joseph II were not forgotten; the more educated functionaries of the Government, who themselves sometimes meddled with imaginary possible reforms, by far preferred the progressive and intellectual despotism of that Emperor to the "paternal" despotism of Metternich. A portion of the poorer nobility equally sided with the middle class, and as to the lower classes of the population, who always had found plenty of grounds to complain of their superiors, if not of the Government, they in most cases could not but adhere to the reformatory wishes of the bourgeoisie.

It was about this time, say 1843 or 1844, that a particular branch of literature, agreeable to this change, was established in Germany. A few Austrian writers, novelists, literary critics, bad poets, the whole of them of very indifferent ability, but gifted with that peculiar industrialism proper to the Jewish race, established themselves in Leipsic and other German towns out of Austria, and there out of the reach of Metternich, published a number of books and pamphlets on Austrian affairs. They and their publishers made " a roaring trade " of it. All Germany was eager to become initiated into the secrets of the policy of European China; and the Austrians themselves, who obtained these publications by the wholesale smuggling carried on upon the Bohemian frontier, were still more curious. Of course the secrets let out in these publications were of no great importance, and the reform plans schemed out by their well-wishing authors bore the stamp of an innocuousness almost amounting to political virginity. A Constitution and a free press for Austria were things considered unattainable; administrative reforms, extension of the rights of the Provincial Diets, admission of foreign books and newspapers, and a less severe censorship—the loyal and humble desires of these good Austrians did hardly go any farther.

At all events the growing impossibility of preventing the literary intercourse of Austria with the rest of Germany, and through Germany with the rest of the world, contributed much toward the formation of an anti-Governmental public opinion, and brought at least some little political information within the reach of part of the Austrian population. Thus, by the end of 1847, Austria was seized, although in an inferior degree, by that political and politico-religious agitation which then prevailed in all Germany; and if its progress in Austria was more silent, it did, nevertheless, find revolutionary elements enough to work upon. There was the peasant, serf, or feudal tenant, ground down into the dust by lordly or Government exactions; then the factory operative, forced by the stick of the policeman to work upon any terms the manufacturer chose to grant; then the journeyman, debarred by the corporative laws from any chance of gaining an independence in his trade; then the merchant, stumbling at every step in business over absurd regulations; then the manufacturer, in uninterrupted conflict with trade guilds, jealous of their privileges, or with greedy and meddling officials; then the schoolmaster, the savant, the better educated functionary, vainly struggling against an ignorant and presumptuous clergy, or a stupid and dictating superior. In short, there was not a single class satisfied, for the small concessions Government was obliged now and then to make were not made at its own expense, for the Treasury could not afford that, but at the expense of the high aristocracy and clergy; and as to the great bankers, and fundholders, the late events in Italy, the increasing opposition of the Hungarian Diet, and the unwonted spirit of discontent and cry for reform, manifesting themselves all over the Empire, were not of a nature to strengthen their faith in the solidity and solvency of the Austrian Empire.

Thus Austria, too, was marching slowly but surely toward a mighty change, when, of a sudden, an event broke out in France, which at once brought down the impending storm, and gave the lie to old Francis's assertion, that the building would hold out both during his and Metternich's lifetime.

New York Daily Tribune, November 7th, 1851.

V

London, October 1851.

ON February 24th, 1848, Louis Philippe was driven out of Paris, and the French Republic was proclaimed. On March 13th following, the people of Vienna broke the power of Prince Metternich, and made him flee shamefully out of the country. On March 18th the people of Berlin rose in arms, and, after an obstinate struggle of eighteen hours, had the satisfaction of seeing the King surrender himself into their hands. Simultaneous outbreaks of a more or less violent nature, but all with the same success, occurred in the capitals of the smaller States of Germany. The German people, if they had not accomplished their first revolution, were at least fairly launched into the revolutionary career.

As to the incidents of these various insurrections, we cannot enter here into the details of them: what we have to explain is their character, and the position which the different classes of the population took up with regard to them.

The Revolution of Vienna may be said to have been made by an almost unanimous population. The bourgeoisie (with the exception of the bankers and stock-jobbers), the petty trading class, the working people, one and all arose at once against a Government detested by all, a Government so universally hated, that the small minority of nobles and money lords which had supported it made itself invisible on the very first attack. The middle classes had been kept in such a degree of political ignorance by Metternich that to them the news from Paris about the reign of Anarchy, Socialism, and terror, and about impending struggles between the class of capitalists and the class of labourers, proved quite unintelligible. They, in their political innocence, either could attach no meaning to these news, or they believed them to be fiendish inventions of Metternich, to frighten them into obedience. They, besides, had never seen working men acting as a class, or stand up for their own distinct class interests. They had, from their past experience, no idea of the possibility of any differences springing up between classes that now were so heartily united in upsetting a Government hated by all. They saw the working people agree with themselves upon all points: a Constitution, Trial by Jury, Liberty of the Press, etc. Thus they were, in March 1848, at least, heart and soul with the movement, and the movement, on the other hand, at once constituted them the (at least in theory) predominant class of the State.

But it is the fate of all revolutions that this union of different classes, which in some degree is always the necessary condition of any revolution, cannot subsist long. No sooner is the victory gained against the common enemy than the victors become divided among themselves into different camps, and turn their weapons against each other. It is this rapid and passionate development of class antagonism which, in old and complicated social organisms, makes a revolution such a powerful agent of social and political progress; it is this incessantly quick upshooting of new parties succeeding each other in power, which, during those violent commotions, makes a nation pass in five years over more ground than it would have done in a century under ordinary circumstances.

The Revolution in Vienna made the middle class the theoretically predominant class; that is to say, the concessions wrung from the Government were such as, once carried out practically and adhered to for a time, would inevitably have secured the supremacy of the middle class. But practically the supremacy of that class was far from being established. It is true that by the establishment of a national guard, which gave arms to the bourgeoisie and petty tradesmen, that class obtained both force and importance; it is true that by the installation of a " Committee of Safety," a sort of revolutionary, irresponsible Government in which the bourgeoisie predominated, it was placed at the head of power. But, at the same time, the working classes were partially armed too; they and the students had borne the brunt of the fight, as far as fight there had been; and the students, about 4,000 strong, well armed, and far better disciplined than the national guard, formed the nucleus, the real strength of the revolutionary force, and were no ways willing to act as a mere instrument in the hands of the Committee of Safety. Though they recognised it, and were even its most enthusiastic supporters, they yet formed a sort of independent and rather turbulent body, deliberating for themselves in the "Anla," keeping an intermediate position between the bourgeoisie and the working classes, preventing by constant agitation things from settling down to the old everyday tranquillity, and very often forcing their resolutions upon the Committee of Safety. The working men, on the other hand, almost entirely thrown out of employment, had to be employed in public works at the expense of the State, and the money for this purpose had, of course, to be taken out of the purse of the taxpayers or out of the chest of the city of Vienna. All this could not but become very unpleasant to the tradesmen of Vienna. The manufactures of the city, calculated for the consumption of the rich and aristocratic courts of a large country, were as a matter of course entirely stopped by the Revolution, by the flight of the aristocracy and Court; trade was at a standstill, and the continuous agitation and excitement kept up by the students and working people was certainly not the means to "restore confidence," as the phrase went. Thus a certain coolness very soon sprung up between the middle classes on the one side and the turbulent students and working people on the other; and if for a long time this coolness was not ripened into open hostility, it was because the Ministry, and particularly the Court, in their impatience to restore the old order of things, constantly justified the suspicions and the turbulent activity of the more revolutionary parties, and constantly made arise, even before the eyes of the middle classes, the spectre of old Metternichian despotism. Thus on May 15th, and again on the 26th, there were fresh risings of all classes in Vienna, on account of the Government having tried to attack, or to undermine, some of the newly-conquered liberties, and on each occasion the alliance between the national guard or armed middle class, the students, and the working men, was again cemented for a time.

As to the other classes of the population, the aristocracy and the money lords had disappeared, and the peasantry were busily engaged everywhere in removing, down to the very last vestiges of feudalism. Thanks to the war in Italy, and the occupation which Vienna and Hungary gave to the Court, they were left at full liberty, and succeeded in their work of liberation in Austria, better than in any other part of Germany. The Austrian Diet had very shortly after only to confirm the steps already practically taken by the peasantry, and whatever else the Government of Prince Schwartzenberg may be enabled to restore, it will never have the power of re-establishing the feudal servitude of the peasantry. And if Austria at the present moment is again comparatively tranquil, and even strong, it is principally because the great majority of the people, the peasants, have been real gainers by the Revolution, and because whatever else has been attacked by the restored Government, those palpable, substantial advantages, conquered by the peasantry, are as yet untouched.

New York Daily Tribune, November 12th, 1851.

VI

London, October 1851.

THE second centre of revolutionary action was Berlin, and from what has been stated in the foregoing papers, it may be guessed that there this action was far from having that unanimous support of almost all classes by which it was accompanied in Vienna. In Prussia, the bourgeoisie had been already involved in actual struggles with the Government; a rupture had been the result of the " United Diet "; a bourgeois revolution was impending, and that revolution might have been, in its first outbreak, quite as unanimous as that of Vienna, had it not been for the Paris Revolution of February. That event precipitated everything, while at the same time it was carried out under a banner totally different from that under which the Prussian bourgeoisie was preparing to defy its Government. The Revolution of February upset, in France, the very same sort of Government which the Prussian bourgeoisie were going to set up in their own country. The Revolution of February announced itself as a revolution of the working classes against the middle classes; it proclaimed the downfall of middle-class government and the emancipation of the working man. Now the Prussian bourgeoisie had, of late, had quite enough of working-class agitation in their own country. After the first terror of the Silesian riots had passed away, they had even tried to give this agitation a turn in their own favour; but they always had retained a salutary horror of revolutionary Socialism and Communism; and, therefore, when they saw men at the head of the Government in Paris whom they considered as the most dangerous enemies of property, order, religion, family, and of the other Penates of the modern bourgeois, they at once experienced a considerable cooling down of their own revolutionary ardour. They knew that the moment must be seized, and that, without the aid of the working masses, they would be defeated; and yet their courage failed them. Thus they sided with the Government in the first partial and provincial outbreaks, tried to keep the people quiet in Berlin, who, during five days, met in crowds before the royal palace to discuss the news and ask for changes in the Government; and when at last, after the news of the downfall of Metternich, the King made some slight concessions, the bourgeoisie considered the Revolution as completed, and went to thank His Majesty for having fulfilled all the wishes of his people. But then followed the attack of the military on the crowd, the barricades, the struggle, and the defeat of royalty. Then everything was changed; the very working classes, which it had been the tendency of the bourgeoisie to keep in the background, had been pushed forward, had fought and conquered, and all at once were conscious of their strength. Restrictions of suffrage, of the Liberty of the Press, of the right to sit on juries, of the right of meeting—restrictions that would have been very agreeable to the bourgeoisie because they would have touched upon such classes as were beneath them—now were no longer possible. The danger of a repetition of the Parisian scenes of " anarchy " was imminent. Before this danger all former differences disappeared. Against the victorious working man, although he had not yet uttered any specific demands for himself, the friends and the foes of many years united, and the alliance between the bourgeoisie and the supporters of the overturned system was concluded upon the very barricades of Berlin. The necessary concessions, but no more than was unavoidable, were to be made; a ministry of the opposition leaders of the United Diet was to be formed, and in return for its services in saving the Crown, it was to have the support of all the props of the old Government, the feudal aristocracy, the bureaucracy, the army. These were the conditions upon which Messrs. Camphausen and Hansemann undertook the formation of a cabinet.

Such was the dread evinced by the new ministers of the aroused masses, that in their eyes every means was good if it only tended to strengthen the shaken foundations of authority. They, poor deluded wretches, thought every danger of a restoration of the old system had passed away; and thus they made use of the whole of the old State machinery for the purpose of restoring " order." Not a single bureaucrat or military officer was dismissed; not the slightest change was made in the old bureaucratic system of administration. These precious constitutional and responsible ministers even restored to their posts those functionaries whom the people, in the first heat of revolutionary ardour, had driven away on account of their former acts of bureaucratic overbearing. There was nothing altered in Prussia but the persons of the ministers; even the ministerial staffs in the different departments were not touched upon, and all the constitutional place-hunters, who had formed the chorus of the newly-elevated rulers, and who had expected their share of power and office, were told to wait until restored stability allowed changes to be operated in the bureaucratic personnel which now were not without danger.

The King, chap-fallen in the highest degree after the insurrection of March 18th, very soon found out that he was quite as necessary to these "Liberal" ministers as they were to him. The throne had been spared by the insurrection; the throne was the last existing obstacle to "anarchy"; the Liberal middle class and its leaders, now in the ministry, had therefore every interest to keep on excellent terms with the Crown. The King, and the reactionary *camarilla* that surrounded him, were not slow in discovering this, and profited by the circumstance in order to fetter the march of the ministry even in those petty reforms that were from time to time intended.

The first care of the ministry was to give a sort of legal appearance to the recent violent changes. The United Diet was convoked in spite of all popular opposition, in order to vote as the legal and constitutional organ of the people a new electoral law for the election of an Assembly, which was to agree with the Crown upon a new Constitution. The elections were to be indirect, the mass of voters electing a number of electors, who then were to choose the representative. In spite of all opposition this system of double elections passed. The United Diet was then asked for a loan of twenty-five millions of dollars, opposed by the popular party, but equally agreed to.

These acts of the ministry gave a most rapid development to the popular, or as it now called itself, the Democratic Party. This party, headed by the petty trading and shopkeeping class, and uniting under its banner, in the beginning of the Revolution, the large majority of the working people, demanded direct and universal suffrage, the same as established in France, a single

Legislative Assembly, and full and open recognition of the Revolution of March 18th, as the base of the new governmental system. The more moderate faction would be satisfied with a thus " democratised ", monarchy, the more advanced demanded the ultimate establishment of the Republic. Both factions agreed in recognising the German National Assembly at Frankfort as the supreme authority of the country, while the Constitutionalists and Reactionaries affected a great horror of the sovereignty of this body, which they professed to consider as utterly revolutionary.

The independent movement of the working classes had, by the Revolution, been broken up for a time. The immediate wants and circumstances of the movement were such as not to allow any of the specific demands of the Proletarian party to be put in the foreground. In fact, as long as the ground was not cleared for the independent action of the working men, as long as direct and universal suffrage was not yet established, as long as the thirty-six larger and smaller States continued to cut up Germany into numberless morsels, what else could the Proletarian party do but watch the—for them all-important—movement of Paris, and struggle in common with the petty shopkeepers for the attainment of those rights, which would allow them to fight afterwards their own battle?

There were only three points, then, by which the Proletarian party in its political action essentially distinguished itself from the petty trading class, or properly so-called Democratic party; firstly, in judging differently the French movement, with regard to which the Democrats attacked, and the Proletarian Revolutionists defended, the extreme party in Paris; secondly, in proclaiming the necessity of establishing a German Republic, one and indivisible, while the very extremest ultras among the Democrats only dared to sigh for a Federative Republic; and thirdly, in showing upon every occasion, that revolutionary boldness and readiness for action, in which any party headed by, and composed principally of petty tradesmen, will always be deficient.

The Proletarian, or really Revolutionary party, succeeded only very gradually in withdrawing the mass of the working people from the influence of the Democrats, whose tail they formed in the beginning of the Revolution. But in due time the

D

indecision, weakness, and cowardice of the Democratic leaders did the rest, and it may now be said to be one of the principal results of the last years' convulsions, that wherever the working class is concerned in anything like considerable masses, they are entirely freed from that Democratic influence which led them into an endless series of blunders and misfortunes during 1848 and 1849. But we had better not anticipate; the events of these two years will give us plenty of opportunities to show the Democratic gentlemen at work.

The peasantry in Prussia, the same as in Austria, but with less energy, feudalism pressing, upon the whole, not quite so hardly upon them here, had profited by the Revolution to free themselves at once from all feudal shackles. But here, from the reasons stated before, the middle classes at once turned against them, their oldest, their most indispensable allies; the Democrats, equally frightened with the bourgeoisie, by what was called attacks upon private property, failed equally to support them; and thus, after three months' emancipation, after bloody struggles and military executions, particularly in Silesia, feudalism was restored by the hands of the, until yesterday, anti-feudal bourgeoisie. There is not a more damning fact to be brought against them than this. Similar treason against its best allies, against itself, never was committed by any party in history, and whatever humiliation and chastisement may be in store for this middle-class party, it has deserved by this one act every morsel of it.

New York Daily Tribune, November 28th, 1851.

VII

London, January 1852.

It will perhaps be in the recollection of our readers that in the six preceding papers we followed up the revolutionary movement of Germany to the two great popular victories of March 13th in Vienna, and March 18th in Berlin. We saw, both in Austria and Prussia, the establishment of Constitutional Governments and the proclamation, as leading rules for all future policy, of Liberal, or middle-class principles; and the only difference observable between the two great centres of action was this, that in Prussia the Liberal bourgeoisie, in the persons of two wealthy merchants, Messrs. Camphausen and Hansemann, directly seized upon the reins of power; while in Austria, where the bourgeoisie was, politically, far less educated, the Liberal bureaucracy walked into office, and professed to hold power in trust for them. We have further seen, how the parties and classes of society, that were heretofore all united in opposition to the old Government, got divided among themselves after the victory, or even during the struggle; and how that same Liberal bourgeoisie that alone profited from the victory turned round immediately upon its allies of yesterday, assumed a hostile attitude against every class or party of a more advanced character, and concluded an alliance with the conquered feudal and bureaucratic interests. It was, in fact, evident, even from the beginning of the revolutionary drama, that the Liberal bourgeoisie could not hold its ground against the vanquished, but not destroyed, feudal and bureaucratic parties except by relying upon the assistance of the popular and more advanced parties; and that it equally required, against the torrent of these more advanced masses, the assistance of the feudal nobility and of the bureaucracy. Thus, it was clear enough that the bourgeoisie in Austria and Prussia did not possess sufficient strength to maintain their power, and to adapt the institutions of the country to their own wants and ideas. The

Liberal bourgeois ministry was only a halting-place from which, according to the turn circumstances might take, the country would either have to go on to the more advanced stage of Unitarian Republicanism, or to relapse into the old clerico-feudal and bureaucratic regime. At all events, the real, decisive struggle was yet to come; the events of March had only engaged the combat.

Austria and Prussia being the two ruling States of Germany, every decisive revolutionary victory in Vienna or Berlin would have been decisive for all Germany. And as far as they went, the events of March 1848, in these two cities, decided the turn of German affairs. It would, then, be superfluous to recur to the movements that occurred in the minor States; and we might, indeed, confine ourselves to the consideration of Austrian and Prussian affairs exclusively, if the existence of these minor States had not given rise to a body which was, by its very existence, a most striking proof of the abnormal situation of Germany and of the incompleteness of the late Revolution; a body so abnormal, so ludicrous by its very position, and yet so full of its own importance, that history will, most likely, never afford a pendant to it. This body was the so-called *German National Assembly* at Frankfort-on-Main.

After the popular victories of Vienna and Berlin, it was a matter of course that there should be a Representative Assembly for all Germany. This body was consequently elected, and met at Frankfort, by the side of the old Federative Diet. The German National Assembly was expected, by the people, to settle every matter in dispute, and to act as the highest legislative authority for the whole of the German Confederation. But, at the same time, the Diet which had convoked it had in no way fixed its attributions. No one knew whether its decrees were to have force of law, or whether they were to be subject to the sanction of the Diet, or of the individual Governments. In this perplexity, if the Assembly had been possessed of the least energy, it would have immediately dissolved and sent home the Diet—than which no corporate body was more unpopular in Germany—and replaced it by a Federal Government, chosen from among its own members. It would have declared itself the only legal expression of the sovereign will of the German people, and thus have attached legal validity to every one of its decrees. It would, above all, have secured to itself an organised and armed force in the country sufficient to put down any opposition on the part of the Governments. And all this was easy, very easy, at that early period of the Revolution. But that would have been expecting a great deal too much from an Assembly composed in its majority of Liberal attorneys and doctrinaire professors, an Assembly which, while it pretended to embody the very essence of German intellect and science, was in reality nothing but a stage where old and worn-out political characters exhibited their involuntary ludicrousness and their impotence of thought, as well as action, before the eyes of all Germany. This Assembly of old women was, from the first day of its existence, more frightened of the least popular movement than of all the reactionary plots of all the German Governments put together. It deliberated under the eyes of the Diet, nay, it almost craved the Diet's sanction to its decrees, for its first resolutions had to be promulgated by that odious body. Instead of asserting its own sovereignty, it studiously avoided the discussion of any such dangerous question. Instead of surrounding itself by a popular force, it passed to the order of the day over all the violent encroachments of the Governments; Mayence, under its very eyes, was placed in a state of siege, and the people there disarmed, and the National Assembly did not stir. Later on it elected Archduke John of Austria Regent of Germany, and declared that all its resolutions were to have the force of law; but then Archduke John was only instituted in his new dignity after the consent of all the Governments had been obtained, and he was instituted not by the Assembly, but by the Diet; and as to the legal force of the decrees of the Assembly, that point was never recognised by the larger Governments, nor enforced by the Assembly itself; it therefore remained in suspense. Thus we had the strange spectacle of an Assembly pretending to be the only legal representative of a great and sovereign nation, and yet never possessing either the will or the force to make its claims recognised. The debates of this body, without any practical result, were not even of any theoretical value, reproducing, as they did, nothing but the most hackneyed commonplace themes of superannuated philosophical and juridical schools; every sentence that was said, or rather stammered forth, in that Assembly having been printed a thousand times over, and a thousand times better, long before.

GERMANY

Thus the pretended new central authority of Germany left everything as it had found it. So far from realising the long-demanded unity of Germany, it did not dispossess the most insignificant of the princes who ruled her; it did not draw closer the bonds of union between her separated provinces; it never moved a single step to break down the custom-house barriers that separated Hanover from Prussia, and Prussia from Austria; it did not even make the slightest attempt to remove the obnoxious dues that everywhere obstruct river navigation in Prussia. But the less this Assembly did the more it blustered. It created a German Fleet—upon paper; it annexed Poland and Schleswig; it allowed German-Austria to carry on war against Italy, and yet prohibited the Italians from following up the Austrians into their safe retreat in Germany; it gave three cheers and one cheer more for the French Republic, and it received Hungarian embassies, which certainly went home with far more confused ideas about Germany than they had come with.

This Assembly had been, in the beginning of the Revolution, the bugbear of all German Governments. They had counted upon a very dictatorial and revolutionary action on its part—on account of the very want of definiteness in which it had been found necessary to leave its competency. These Governments, therefore, got up a most comprehensive system of intrigues in order to weaken the influence of this dreaded body; but they proved to have more luck than wits, for this Assembly did the work of the Governments better than they themselves could have done. The chief feature among these intrigues was the convocation of local Legislative Assemblies, and in consequence, not only the lesser States convoked their Legislatures, but Prussia and Austria also called Constituent Assemblies. In these, as in the Frankfort House of Representatives, the Liberal middle class, or its allies, Liberal lawyers, and bureaucrats had the majority, and the turn affairs took in each of them was nearly the same. The only difference is this, that the German National Assembly was the Parliament of an imaginary country, as it had declined the task of forming what nevertheless was its own first condition of existence, viz., a United Germany; that it discussed the imaginary and never-to-be-carried-out measures of an imaginary Government of its own creation, and that it passed imaginary resolutions for which nobody cared; while in Austria and Prussia the constituent bodies were at least real parliaments, upsetting and creating real ministries, and forcing, for a time at least, their resolutions upon the princes with whom they had to contend. They, too, were cowardly, and lacked enlarged views of revolutionary resolutions; they, too, betrayed the people, and restored power to the hands of feudal, bureaucratic, and military despotism. But then they were at least obliged to discuss practical questions of immediate interest, and to live upon earth with other people, while the Frankfort humbugs were never happier than when they could roam in " the airy realms of dream," *im Luftreich des Traums*. Thus the proceedings of the Berlin and Vienna Constituents form an important part of German revolutionary history, while the lucubrations of the Frankfort collective tomfoolery merely interest the collector of literary and antiquarian curiosities.

The people of Germany, deeply feeling the necessity of doing away with the obnoxious territorial division that scattered and annihilated the collective force of the nation, for some time expected to find, in the Frankfort National Assembly at least, the beginning of a new era. But the childish conduct of that set of wiseacres soon disenchanted the national enthusiasm. The disgraceful proceedings occasioned by the armistice of Malmoe (September 1848) made the popular indignation burst out against a body which, it had been hoped, would give the nation a fair field for action, and which, instead, carried away by unequalled cowardice, only restored to their former solidity the foundations upon which the present counter-revolutionary system is built.

New York Daily Tribune, February 27th, 1852.

VIII

London, February 1852.

FROM what has been stated in the foregoing articles, it is already evident that unless a fresh revolution was to follow that of March 1848, things would inevitably return, in Germany, to what they were before this event. But such is the complicated nature of the historical theme upon which we are trying to throw some light, that subsequent events cannot be clearly understood without taking into account what may be called the foreign relations of the German Revolution. And these foreign relations were of the same intricate nature as the home affairs.

The whole of the eastern half of Germany, as far as the Elbe, Saale, and Bohemian Forest, has, it is well known, been reconquered during the last thousand years, from invaders of Slavonic origin. The greater part of these territories have been Germanised, to the perfect extinction of all Slavonic nationality and language for several centuries past; and if we except a few totally isolated remnants, amounting in the aggregate to less than a hundred thousand souls (Kassubians in Pomerania, Wends or Sorbians in Lusatia), their inhabitants are, to all intents and purposes, Germans. But the case is different along the whole of the frontier of ancient Poland, and in the countries of the Tschechian tongue, in Bohemia and Moravia. Here the two nationalities are mixed up in every district, the towns being generally more or less German, while the Slavonic element prevails in the rural villages, where, however, it is also gradually disintegrated and forced back by the steady advance of German influence.

The reason of this state of things is this: ever since the time of Charlemagne, the Germans have directed their most constant and persevering efforts to the conquest, colonisation, or, at least, civilisation of the east of Europe. The conquests of the feudal nobility between the Elbe and the Oder, and the feudal colonies of the military orders of knights in Prussia and Livonia, only laid the ground for a far more extensive and effective system of Germanisation by the trading and manufacturing middle classes, which in Germany, as in the rest of Western Europe, rose into social and political importance since the fifteenth century. The Slavonians, and particularly the Western Slavonians (Poles and Tschechs), are essentially an agricultural race; trade and manufactures never were in great favour with them. The consequence was that, with the increase of population and the origin of cities in these regions, the production of all articles of manufacture fell into the hands of German immigrants, and the exchange of these commodities against agricultural produce became the exclusive monopoly of the Jews, who, if they belong to any nationality, are in these countries certainly rather Germans than Slavonians. This has been, though in a less degree, the case in all the east of Europe. The handicraftsman, the small shopkeeper, the petty manufacturer, is a German up to this day in Petersburg, Pesth, Jassy, and even Constantinople; while the money-lender, the publican, the hawker—a very important man in these thinly populated countries—is very generally a Jew, whose native tongue is a horribly corrupted German. The importance of the German element in the Slavonic frontier localities, thus rising with the growth of towns, trade, and manufactures, was still increased when it was found necessary to import almost every element of mental culture from Germany; after the German merchant and handicraftsman, the German clergyman, the German schoolmaster, the German savant came to establish himself upon Slavonic soil. And lastly, the iron tread of conquering armies, or the cautious, well-premeditated grasp of diplomacy, not only followed, but many times went ahead of the slow but sure advance of denationalisation by social developments. Thus, great parts of Western Prussia and Posen have been Germanised since the first partition of Poland, by sales and grants of public domains to German colonists, by encouragements given to German capitalists for the establishment of manufactories, etc., in those neighbourhoods, and very often, too, by excessively despotic measures against the Polish inhabitants of the country.

In this manner the last seventy years had entirely changed the line of demarcation between the German and Polish nationalities. The Revolution of 1848 calling forth at once the claim of all oppressed nations to an independent existence, and to the right of settling their own affairs for themselves, it was quite natural that the Poles should at once demand the restoration of their country within the frontiers of the old Polish Republic before 1772. It is true, this frontier, even at that time, had become obsolete, if taken as the delimitation of German and Polish nationality; it had become more so every year since by the progress of Germanisation; but then, the Germans had proclaimed such an enthusiasm for the restoration of Poland, that they must expect to be asked, as a first proof of the reality of their sympathies, to give up *their* share of the plunder. On the other hand, should whole tracts of land, inhabited chiefly by Germans, should large towns, entirely German, be given up to a people that as yet had never given any proofs of its capability of progressing beyond a state of feudalism based upon agricultural serfdom ? The question was intricate enough. The only possible solution was in a war with Russia. The question of delimitation between the different revolutionised nations would have been made a secondary one to that of first establishing a safe frontier against the common enemy.. The Poles, by receiving extended territories in the east, would have become more tractable and reasonable in the west, and Riga and Memel would have been deemed, after all, quite as important to them as Danzig and Elbing. Thus the advanced party in Germany, deeming a war with Russia necessary to keep up the Continental movement, and considering that the national re-establishment even of a part of Poland would inevitably lead to such a war, supported the Poles; while the reigning middle-class party clearly foresaw its downfall from any national war against Russia, which would have called more active and energetic men to the helm, and, therefore, with a feigned enthusiasm for the extension of German nationality, they declared Prussian Poland, the chief seat of Polish revolutionary agitation, to be part and parcel of the German Empire that was to be. The promises given to the Poles in the first days of excitement were shamefully broken. Polish armaments got up with the sanction of the Government were dispersed and massacred by Prussian artillery; and as soon as the month of April 1848, within six weeks of the Berlin Revolution, the Polish movement was crushed, and the old national hostility revived between Poles and Germans. This immense and incalculable service to the Russian autocrat was performed by the Liberal merchant-ministers,

Camphausen and Hansemann. It must be added that this Polish campaign was the first means of reorganising and reassuring that same Prussian army, which afterward turned out the Liberal party, and crushed the movement which Messrs. Camphausen and Hansemann had taken such pains to bring about. " Whereby they sinned, thereby are they punished." Such has been the fate of all the upstarts of 1848 and 1849, from Ledru Rollin to Changarnier, and from Camphausen down to Haynau.

The question of nationality gave rise to another struggle in Bohemia. This country, inhabited by two millions of Germans, and three millions of Slavonians of the Tschechian tongue, had great historical recollections, almost all connected with the former supremacy of the Tschechs. But then the force of this branch of the Slavonic family had been broken ever since the wars of the Hussites in the fifteenth century. The province speaking the Tschechian tongue was divided, one part forming the kingdom of Bohemia, another the principality of Moravia, a third the Carpathian hill-country of the Slovaks, being part of Hungary. The Moravians and Slovaks had long since lost every vestige of national feeling and vitality, although mostly preserving their language. Bohemia was surrounded by thoroughly German countries on three sides out of four. The German element had made great progress on her own territory; even in the capital, in Prague, the two nationalities were pretty equally matched; and everywhere capital, trade, industry, and mental culture were in the hands of the Germans. The chief champion of the Tschechian nationality, Professor Palacky, is himself nothing but a learned German run mad, who even now cannot speak the Tschechian language correctly and without foreign accent. But as it often happens, dying Tschechian nationality, dying according to every fact known in history for the last four hundred years, made in 1848 a last effort to regain its former vitality—an effort whose failure, independently of all revolutionary considerations, was to prove that Bohemia could only exist henceforth, as a portion of Germany, although part of her inhabitants might yet, for some centuries, continue to speak a non-German language.

New York Daily Tribune, March 5th, 1852.

IX

London, February 1852.

BOHEMIA and Croatia (another disjected member of the Slavonic family, acted upon by the Hungarian, as Bohemia by the German) were the homes of what is called on the European continent "Panslavism." Neither Bohemia nor Croatia was strong enough to exist as a nation by herself. Their respective nationalities, gradually undermined by the action of historical causes that inevitably absorbs into a more energetic stock, could only hope to be restored to anything like independence by an alliance with other Slavonic nations. There were twenty-two millions of Poles, forty-five millions of Russians, eight millions of Serbians and Bulgarians; why not form a mighty confederation of the whole eighty millions of Slavonians, and drive back or exterminate the intruder upon the holy Slavonic soil, the Turk, the Hungarian, and above all the hated, but indispensable *Niemetz*, the German ? Thus in the studies of a few Slavonian *dilettanti* of historical science was this ludicrous, this anti-historical movement got up, a movement which intended nothing less than to subjugate the civilised West under the barbarian East, the town under the country, trade, manufactures, intelligence, under the primitive agriculture of Slavonian serfs. But behind this ludicrous theory stood the terrible reality of the *Russian Empire*; that empire which by every movement proclaims the pretension of considering all Europe as the domain of the Slavonic race, and especially of the only energetic part of this race, of the Russians; that empire which, with two capitals such as St. Petersburg and Moscow, has not yet found its centre of gravity, as long as the "City of the Czar" (Constantinople, called in Russian Tzarigrad, the Czar's city), considered by every Russian peasant as the true metropolis of his religion and his nation, is not actually the residence of its Emperor; that empire which, for the last one hundred and fifty years, has never lost, but always gained territory by every war it has commenced. And well known in Central Europe are the intrigues by which Russian policy supported the new-fangled system of Panslavism, a system than which none better could be invented to suit its purposes. Thus, the Bohemian and Croatian Panslavists, some intentionally, some without knowing it, worked in the direct interest of Russia; they betrayed the revolutionary cause for the shadow of a nationality which, in the best of cases, would have shared the fate of the Polish nationality under Russian sway. It must, however, be said for the honour of the Poles, that they never get to be seriously entangled in these Panslavist traps, and if a few of the aristocracy turned furious Panslavists, they knew that by Russian subjugation they had less to lose than by a revolt of their own peasant serfs.

The Bohemians and Croatians called, then, a general Slavonic Congress at Prague, for the preparation of the universal Slavonian Alliance. This Congress would have proved a decided failure even without the interference of the Austrian military. The several Slavonic languages differ quite as much as the English, the German, and the Swedish, and when the proceedings opened, there was no common Slavonic tongue by which the speakers could make themselves understood. French was tried, but was equally unintelligible to the majority, and the poor Slavonic enthusiasts, whose only common feeling was a common hatred against the Germans, were at last obliged to express themselves in the hated German language, as the only one that was generally understood! But just then another Slavonic Congress was assembling in Prague, in the shape of Galician lancers, Croatian and Slovak grenadiers, and Bohemian gunners and cuirassiers; and this real, armed Slavonic Congress, under the command of Windischgrätz, in less than twenty-four hours drove the founders of an imaginary Slavonic supremacy out of the town, and dispersed them to the winds.

The Bohemian, Moravian, Dalmatian, and part of the Polish deputies (the aristocracy) to the Austrian Constituent Diet, made in that Assembly a systematic war upon the German element. The Germans, and part of the Poles (the impoverished nobility), were in this Assembly the chief supporters of revolutionary progress; the mass of the Slavonic deputies, in opposing them, were not satisfied with thus showing clearly the reactionary tendencies of their entire movement, but they were degraded enough to tamper and conspire with the very same Austrian Government which had dispersed their meeting at Prague. They, too, were paid for this infamous conduct; after supporting the Government during the insurrection of October 1848, an event which finally secured to them a majority in the Diet, this now almost exclusively Slavonic Diet was dispersed by Austrian soldiers, the same as the Prague Congress, and the Panslavists threatened with imprisonment if they should stir again. And they have only obtained this, that Slavonic nationality is now being everywhere undermined by Austrian centralisation, a result for which they may thank their own fanaticism and blindness.

If the frontiers of Hungary and Germany had admitted of any doubt, there would certainly have been another quarrel there. But, fortunately, there was no pretext, and the interests of both nations being intimately related, they struggled against the same enemies, viz., the Austrian Government and the Panslavistic fanaticism. The good understanding was not for a moment disturbed. But the Italian Revolution entangled at least a part of Germany in an internecine war, and it must be stated here, as a proof how far the Metternichian system had succeeded in keeping back the development of the public mind, that during the first six months of 1848, the same men that had in Vienna mounted the barricades, went, full of enthusiasm, to join the army that fought against the Italian patriots. This deplorable confusion of ideas did not, however, last long.

Lastly, there was the war with Denmark about Schleswig and Holstein. These countries, unquestionably German by nationality, language and predilection, are also from military, naval and commercial grounds necessary to Germany. Their inhabitants have, for the last three years, struggled hard against Danish intrusion. The right of treaties, besides, was for them. The Revolution of March brought them into open collision with the Danes, and Germany supported them. But while in Poland, in Italy, in Bohemia, and later on, in Hungary, military operations were pushed with the utmost vigour, in this the only popular, the only, at least partially, revolutionary war, a system of resultless marches and counter-marches was adopted, and an interference of foreign diplomacy was submitted to, which led, after many an heroic engagement, to a most miserable end. The German Government betrayed, during the war, the Schleswig-Holstein revolutionary army on every occasion, and allowed it purposely to be cut up, when dispersed or divided, by the Danes. The German corps of volunteers were treated the same.

But while thus the German name earned nothing but hatred on every side, the German Constitutional and Liberal Governments rubbed their hands for joy. They had succeeded in crushing the Polish and Bohemian movements. They had everywhere revived the old national animosities, which heretofore had prevented any common understanding and action between the German, the Pole, the Italian. They had accustomed the people to scenes of civil war and repression by the military. The Prussian army had regained its confidence in Poland, the Austrian army in Prague; and while the superabundant patriotism ("*die Patriotische Ueberkraft,*" as Heine has it) of revolutionary but short-sighted youth was led in Schleswig and Lombardy, to be crushed by the grape-shot of the enemy, the regular army, the real instrument of action, both of Prussia and Austria, was placed in a position to regain public favour by victories over the foreigner. But we repeat: these armies, strengthened by the Liberals as a means of action against the more advanced party, no sooner had recovered their self-confidence and their discipline in some degree, than they turned themselves against the Liberals, and restored to power the men of the old system. When Radetzky, in his camp beyond the Adige, received the first orders from the " responsible ministers " at Vienna, he exclaimed: " Who are these ministers ? They are not the Government of Austria! Austria is now nowhere but in my camp; I and my army, we are Austria; and when we shall have beaten the Italians we shall reconquer the Empire for the Emperor! " And old Radetzky was right—but the imbecile " responsible " ministers at Vienna heeded him not.

New York Daily Tribune, March 15th, 1852.

X

London, February 1852.

As early as the beginning of April 1848, the revolutionary torrent had found itself stemmed all over the Continent of Europe by the league which those classes of society that had profited by the first victory immediately formed with the vanquished. In France, the petty trading class and the Republican faction of the bourgeoisie had combined with the Monarchist bourgeoisie against the proletarians; in Germany and Italy, the victorious bourgeoisie had eagerly courted the support of the feudal nobility, the official bureaucracy, and the army, against the mass of the people and the petty traders. Very soon the united Conservative and Counter-Revolutionary parties again regained the ascendant. In England, an untimely and ill-prepared popular demonstration (April 10th) turned out a complete and decisive defeat of the popular party. In France, two similar movements (April 16th and May 15th) were equally defeated. In Italy, King Bomba regained his authority by a single stroke on May 15th. In Germany, the different new bourgeois Governments and their respective constituent Assemblies consolidated themselves, and if the eventful May 15th gave rise, in Vienna, to a popular victory, this was an event of merely secondary importance, and may be considered the last successful flash of popular energy. In Hungary the movement appeared to turn into the quiet channel of perfect legality, and the Polish movement, as we have seen in our last, was stifled in the bud by Prussian bayonets. But as yet nothing was decided as to the eventual turn which things would take, and every inch of ground lost by the Revolutionary parties in the different countries only tended to close their ranks more and more for the decisive action.

The decisive action drew near. It could be fought in France only; for France, as long as England took no part in the revolutionary strife, or as Germany remained divided, was, by its national independence, civilisation, and centralisation, the only country to impart the impulse of a mighty convulsion to the surrounding countries. Accordingly, when, on June 23rd, 1848, the bloody struggle began in Paris, when every succeeding telegraph or mail more clearly exposed the fact to the eyes of Europe, that this struggle was carried on between the mass of the working people on the one hand, and all the other classes of the Parisian population, supported by the army, on the other; when the fighting went on for several days with an exasperation unequalled in the history of modern civil warfare, but without any apparent advantage for either side—then it became evident to every one that this was the great decisive battle which would, if the insurrection were victorious, deluge the whole continent with renewed revolutions, or, if it was suppressed, bring about an at least momentary restoration of counter-revolutionary rule.

The proletarians of Paris were defeated, decimated, crushed with such an effect that even now they have not yet recovered from the blow. And immediately, all over Europe, the new and old Conservatives and Counter-Revolutionists raised their heads with an effrontery that showed how well they understood the importance of the event. The Press was everywhere attacked, the rights of meeting and association were interfered with, every little event in every small provincial town was taken profit of to disarm the people to declare a state of siege, to drill the troops in the new manœuvres and artifices that Cavaignac had taught them. Besides, for the first time since February, the invincibility of a popular insurrection in a large town had been proved to be a delusion; the honour of the armies had been restored; the troops hitherto always defeated in street battles of importance regained confidence in their efficiency even in this kind of struggle.

From this defeat of the *ouvriers* of Paris may be dated the first positive steps and definite plans of the old feudal bureaucratic party in Germany, to get rid even of their momentary allies, the middle classes, and to restore Germany to the state she was in before the events of March. The army again was the decisive power in the State, and the army belonged not to the middle classes but to themselves. Even in Prussia, where before 1848 a considerable leaning of part of the lower grades of officers towards

E

a Constitutional Government had been observed, the disorder introduced into the army by the Revolution had brought back those reasoning young men to their allegiance; as soon as the private soldier took a few liberties with regard to the officers, the necessity of discipline and passive obedience became at once strikingly evident to them. The vanquished nobles and bureaucrats now began to see their way before them; the army, more united than ever, flushed with victory in minor insurrections and in foreign warfare, jealous of the great success the French soldiers had just attained—this army had only to be kept in constant petty conflicts with the people, and the decisive moment once at hand, it could with one great blow crush the Revolutionists, and set aside the presumptions of the middle-class Parliamentarians. And the proper moment for such a decisive blow arrived soon enough.

We pass over the sometimes curious, but mostly tedious, parliamentary proceedings and local struggles that occupied, in Germany, the different parties during the summer. Suffice it to say that the supporters of the middle-class interest in spite of numerous parliamentary triumphs, not one of which led to any practical result, very generally felt that their position between the extreme parties became daily more untenable, and that, therefore, they were obliged now to seek the alliance of the reactionists, and the next day to court the favour of the more popular factions. This constant vacillation gave the finishing stroke to their character in public opinion, and according to the turn events were taking, the contempt into which they had sunk, profited for the movement principally to the bureaucrats and feudalists.

By the beginning of autumn the relative position of the different parties had become exasperated and critical enough to make a decisive battle inevitable. The first engagements in this war between the democratic and revolutionary masses and the army took place at Frankfort. Though a mere secondary engagement, it was the first advantage of any note the troops acquired over the insurrection, and had a great moral effect. The fancy Government established by the Frankfort National Assembly had been allowed by Prussia, for very obvious reasons, to conclude an armistice with Denmark, which not only surrendered to Danish vengeance the Germans of Schleswig, but which also entirely disclaimed the more or less revolutionary principles which were generally supposed in the Danish war. This armistice was, by a majority of two or three, rejected in the Frankfort Assembly. A sham ministerial crisis followed this vote, but three days later the Assembly reconsidered their vote, and were actually induced to cancel it and acknowledge the armistice. This disgraceful proceeding roused the indignation of the people. Barricades were erected, but already sufficient troops had been drawn to Frankfort, and after six hours' fighting, the insurrection was suppressed. Similar, but less important, movements connected with this event took place in other parts of Germany (Baden, Cologne), but were equally defeated.

This preliminary engagement gave to the Counter-Revolutionary party the one great advantage, that now the only Government which had entirely—at least in semblance—originated with popular election, the Imperial Government of Frankfort, as well as the National Assembly, was ruined in the eyes of the people. This Government and this Assembly had been obliged to appeal to the bayonets of the troops against the manifestation of the popular will. They were compromised, and what little regard they might have been hitherto enabled to claim, this repudiation of their origin, the dependency upon the anti-popular Governments and their troops, made both the Lieutenant of the Empire, his ministers and his deputies, henceforth to be complete nullities. We shall soon see how first Austria, then Prussia, and later on the smaller States too, treated with contempt every order, every request, every deputation they received from this body of impotent dreamers.

We now come to the great counter-stroke in Germany, of the French battle of June, to that event which was as decisive for Germany as the proletarian struggle of Paris had been for France; we mean the revolution and subsequent storming of Vienna, October 1848. But the importance of this battle is such, and the explanation of the different circumstances that more immediately contributed to its issue will take up such a portion of the *Tribune's* columns, as to necessitate its being treated in a separate letter.

New York Daily Tribune, March 18th, 1852.

XI

London, March 1852.

WE now come to the decisive events which formed the counter-revolutionary part in Germany to the Parisian insurrection of June, and which, by a single blow, turned the scale in favour of the Counter-Revolutionary party,—the insurrection of October 1848, in Vienna.

We have seen what the position of the different classes was, in Vienna, after the victory of March 12th. We have also seen how the movement of German-Austria was entangled with and impeded by the events in the non-German provinces of Austria. It only remains for us, then, briefly to survey the causes which led to the last and most formidable rising of German-Austria.

The high aristocracy and the stock-jobbing bourgeoisie, which had formed the principal non-official supports of the Metternichian Government, were enabled, even after the events of March, to maintain a predominating influence with the Government, not only by the Court, the army and the bureaucracy, but still more by the horror of "anarchy," which rapidly spread among the middle classes. They very soon ventured a few feelers in the shape of a Press Law, a nondescript Aristocratic Constitution, and an Electoral Law based upon the old division of "estates." The so-called Constitutional ministry, consisting of half Liberal, timid, incapable bureaucrats, on May 14th, even ventured a direct attack upon the revolutionary organisations of the masses by dissolving the Central Committee of Delegates of the National Guard and Academic Legion, a body formed for the express purpose of controlling the Government, and calling out against it, in case of need, the popular forces. But this act only provoked the insurrection of May 15th, by which the Government was forced to acknowledge the Committee, to repeal the Constitution and the Electoral Law, and to grant the power of framing a new Fundamental Law to a Constitutional Diet, elected by universal suffrage. All this was confirmed on the following day by an Imperial proclamation. But the reactionary party, which also had its representatives in the ministry, soon got their " Liberal " colleagues to undertake a new attack upon the popular conquests. The Academic Legion, the stronghold of the movement party, the centre of continuous agitation, had, on this very account, become obnoxious to the more moderate burghers of Vienna; on the 26th a ministerial decree dissolved it. Perhaps this blow might have succeeded, if it had been carried out by a part of the National Guard only, but the Government, not trusting them either, brought the military forward, and at once the National Guard turned round, united with the Academic Legion, and thus frustrated the ministerial project.

In the meantime, however, the Emperor and his Court had, on May 16th, left Vienna, and fled to Innspruck. Here, surrounded by the bigoted Tyroleans, whose loyalty was roused again by the danger of an invasion of their country by the Sardo-Lombardian army, supported by the vicinity of Radetzky's troops, within shell-range of whom Innspruck lay, here the Counter-Revolutionary party found an asylum, from whence, uncontrolled, unobserved and safe, it might rally its scattered forces, repair and spread again all over the country the network of its plots. Communications were reopened with Radetzky, with Jellachich, and with Windischgrätz, as well as with the reliable men in the administrative hierarchy of the different provinces; intrigues were set on foot with the Slavonic chiefs, and thus a real force at the disposal of the Counter-Revolutionary *camarilla* was formed, while the impotent ministers in Vienna were allowed to wear their short and feeble popularity out in continual bickerings with the revolutionary masses, and in the debates of the forthcoming Constituent Assembly. Thus the policy of leaving the movement of the capital to itself for a time; a policy which must have led to the omnipotence of the movement party in a centralised and homogeneous country like France, here in Austria, in heterogeneous political conglomerate, was one of the safest means of reorganising the strength of the reactionists.

In Vienna the middle class, persuaded that after three successive defeats, and in the face of a Constituent Assembly based upon universal suffrage, the Court was no longer an opponent to be dreaded, fell more and more into that weariness and apathy, and that eternal outcry for order and tranquillity, which has everywhere seized this class after violent commotions and consequent derangement of trade. The manufactures of the Austrian capital are almost exclusively limited to articles of luxury, for which, since the Revolution and the flight of the Court, there had necessarily been little demand. The shout for a return to a regular system of government, and for a return of the Court, both of which were expected to bring about a revival of commercial prosperity—this shout became now general among the middle classes. The meeting of the Constituent Assembly in July was hailed with delight as the end of the revolutionary era; so was the return of the Court, which, after the victories of Radetzky in Italy, and after the advent of the reactionary ministry of Doblhoff, considered itself strong enough to brave the popular torrent, and which, at the same time, was wanted in Vienna in order to complete its intrigues with the Slavonic majority of the Diet. While the Constituent Diet discussed the laws on the emancipation of the peasantry from feudal bondage and forced labour for the nobility, the Court completed a master stroke. On August 19th the Emperor was made to review the National Guard; the Imperial family, the courtiers, the general officers, outbade each other in flatteries to the armed burghers who were already intoxicated with pride at thus seeing themselves publicly acknowledged as one of the important bodies of the State; and immediately afterwards a decree, signed by Herr Schwarzer, the only popular minister in the Cabinet, was published, withdrawing the Government aid, given hitherto to the workmen out of employ. The trick succeeded; the working classes got up a demonstration; the middle-class National Guards declared for the decree of their minister; they were launched upon the " Anarchists," fell like tigers on the unarmed and unresisting workpeople, and massacred a great number of them on August 23rd. Thus the unity and strength of the revolutionary force was broken; the class-struggle between bourgeois and proletarian had come in Vienna, too, to a bloody outbreak, and the counter-revolutionary *camarilla* saw the day approaching on which it might strike its grand blow.

The Hungarian affairs very soon offered an opportunity to proclaim openly the principles upon which it intended to act. On October 5th an Imperial decree in the *Vienna Gazette*—a decree countersigned by none of the responsible ministers for Hungary—declared the Hungarian Diet dissolved, and named the Ban Jellachich, of Croatia, Civil and Military Governor of that country—Jellachich, the leader of South Slavonian reaction, a man who was actually at war with the lawful authorities of Hungary. At the same time orders were given to the troops in Vienna to march out and form part of the army which was to enforce Jellachich's authority. This, however, was showing the cloven foot too openly; every man in Vienna felt that war upon Hungary was war upon the principle of Constitutional Government, which principle was in the very decree trampled upon by the attempt of the Emperor to make decrees with legal force, without the countersign of a responsible minister. The people, the Academic Legion, the National Guard of Vienna, on October 6th rose in mass, and resisted the departure of the troops; some grenadiers passed over to the people, a short struggle took place between the popular forces and the troops; the Minister of War, Latour, was massacred by the people, and in the evening the latter were victors. In the meantime, Ban Jellachich, beaten at Stuhlweissenburg by Perczel, had taken refuge near Vienna on German-Austrian territory; the Viennese troops that were to march to his support now took up an ostensibly hostile and defensive position against him; and the Emperor and Court had again fled to Olmütz, on semi-Slavonic territory.

But at Olmütz the Court found itself in very different circumstances from what it had been at Innspruck. It was now in a position to open immediately the campaign against the Revolution. It was surrounded by the Slavonian deputies of the Constituent, who flocked in masses to Olmütz, and by the Slavonian enthusiasts from all parts of the monarchy. The campaign, in their eyes, was to be a war of Slavonian restoration and of extermination, against the two intruders, upon what was considered Slavonian soil, against the German and the Magyar. Windischgrätz, the conqueror of Prague, now commander of the army that was concentrated around Vienna, became at once the hero of Slavonian nationality. And his army concentrated rapidly from all sides. From Bohemia, Moravia, Styria, Upper Austria, and Italy, marched regiment after regiment on routes that converged at Vienna, to join the troops of Jellachich and the ex-garrison of the capital. Above sixty thousand men were thus united towards the end of October, and soon they commenced hemming in the Imperial city on all sides, until, on October 30th, they were far enough advanced to venture upon the decisive attack.

In Vienna, in the meantime, confusion and helplessness was prevalent. The middle class, as soon as the victory was gained, became again possessed of their old distrust against the " anarchic " working classes; the working men, mindful of the treatment they had received, six weeks before, at the hands of the armed tradesmen, and of the unsteady, wavering policy of the middle class at large, would not trust to them the defence of the city, and demanded arms and military organisation for themselves. The Academic Legion, full of zeal for the struggle against Imperial despotism, were entirely incapable of understanding the nature of the estrangement of the two classes, or of otherwise comprehending the necessities of the situation. There was confusion in the public mind, confusion in the ruling councils. The remnant of the German Diet deputies, and a few Slavonians, acting the part of spies for their friends at Olmütz, besides a few of the more revolutionary Polish deputies, sat in permanency; but instead of taking part resolutely, they lost all their time in idle debates upon the possibility of resisting the Imperial army without overstepping the bounds of constitutional conventionalities. The Committee of Safety, composed of deputies from almost all the popular bodies of Vienna, although resolved to resist, was yet dominated by a majority of burghers and petty tradesmen, who never allowed it to follow up any determined, energetic line of action. The Council of the Academic Legion passed heroic resolutions, but was no ways able to take the lead. The working classes, distrusted, disarmed, disorganised, hardly emerging from the intellectual bondage of the old regime, hardly awaking, not to a knowledge, but to a mere instinct of their social position and proper political line of action, could only make themselves heard by loud demonstrations, and could not be expected to be up to the difficulties of the moment. But they were ready—as they ever were in Germany during the Revolution—to fight to the last, as soon as they obtained arms.

That was the state of things in Vienna. Outside, the reorganised Austrian army flushed with the victories of Radetzky in Italy; sixty or seventy thousand men well armed, well organised, and if not well commanded at least possessing commanders. Inside, confusion, class division, disorganisation; a National Guard part of which was resolved not to fight at all, part irresolute, and only the smallest part ready to act; a proletarian mass, powerful by numbers but without leaders, without any political education, subject to panic as well as to fits of fury almost without cause, a prey to every false rumour spread about, quite ready to fight, but unarmed, at least in the beginning, and incompletely armed, and barely organised when at last they were led to battle; a helpless Diet, discussing theoretical quibbles while the roof over their heads was almost burning; a leading Committee without impulse or energy. Everything was changed from the days of March and May, when, in the Counter-Revolutionary camp, all was confusion, and when the only organised force was that created by the Revolution. There could hardly be a doubt about the issue of such a struggle, and whatever doubt there might be, was settled by the events of October 30th and 31st, and November 1st.

New York Daily Tribune, March 19th, 1852.

XII

London, March 1852.

WHEN at last the concentrated army of Windischgrätz commenced the attack upon Vienna, the forces that could be brought forward in defence were exceedingly insufficient for the purpose. Of the National Guard only a portion was to be brought to the entrenchments. A Proletarian Guard, it is true, had at last been hastily formed, but owing to the lateness of the attempt to thus make available the most numerous, most daring, and most energetic part of the population, it was too little inured to the use of arms and to the very first rudiments of discipline to offer a successful resistance. Thus the Academic Legion, three to four thousand strong, well exercised and disciplined to a certain degree, brave and enthusiastic, was, militarily speaking, the only force which was in a state to do its work successfully. But what were they, together with the few reliable National Guards, and with the confused mass of the armed proletarians, in opposition to the far more numerous regulars of Windischgrätz, not counting even the brigand hordes of Jellachich, hordes that were, by the very nature of their habits, very useful in a war from house to house, from lane to lane? And what but a few old, out-worn, ill-mounted, and ill-served pieces of ordnance had the insurgents to oppose to that numerous and well-appointed artillery, of which Windischgrätz made such an unscrupulous use?

The nearer the danger drew, the more grew the confusion in Vienna. The Diet, up to the last moment, could not collect sufficient energy to call in for aid the Hungarian army of Perczel, encamped a few leagues below the capital. The Committee passed contradictory resolutions, they themselves being, like the popular armed masses, floated up and down with the alternately rising and receding tide of rumours and counter-rumours. There was only one thing upon which all agreed—to respect property; and this was done in a degree almost ludicrous for such times. As to the final arrangement of a plan of defence, very little was done. Bem, the only man present who could have saved Vienna, if any could then in Vienna, an almost unknown foreigner, a Slavonian by birth, gave up the task, overwhelmed as he was by universal distrust. Had he persevered, he might have been lynched as a traitor. Messenhauser, the commander of the insurgent forces, more of a novel-writer than even of a subaltern officer, was totally inadequate to the task; and yet, after eight months of revolutionary struggles, the popular party had not produced or acquired a military man of more ability than he. Thus the contest began. The Viennese, considering their utterly inadequate means of defence, considering their utter absence of military skill and organisation in the ranks, offered a most heroic resistance. In many places the order given by Bem, when he was in command, " to defend that post to the last man," was carried out to the letter. But force prevailed. Barricade after barricade was swept away by the Imperial artillery in the long and wide avenues which form the main streets of the suburbs; and on the evening of the second day's fighting the Croats occupied the range of houses facing the glacis of the Old Town. A feeble and disorderly attack of the Hungarian army had been utterly defeated; and during an armistice, while some parties in the Old Town capitulated, while others hesitated and spread confusion, while the remnants of the Academic Legion prepared fresh entrenchments, an entrance was made by the Imperialists, and in the midst of the general disorder the Old Town was carried.

The immediate consequences of this victory, the brutalities and executions by martial law, the unheard-of cruelties and infamies committed by the Slavonian hordes let loose upon Vienna, are too well known to be detailed here. The ulterior consequences, the entirely new turn given to German affairs by the defeat of the Revolution in Vienna, we shall have reason to notice hereafter. There remain two points to be considered in connection with the storming of Vienna. The people of that capital had two allies— the Hungarians and the German people. Where were they in the hour of trial ?

We have seen that the Viennese, with all the generosity of a newly freed people, had risen for a cause which, though ultimately their own, was, in the first instance, and above all, that of the

Hungarians. Rather than suffer the Austrian troops to march upon Hungary, they would draw their first and most terrific onslaught upon themselves. And while they thus nobly came forward for the support of their allies, the Hungarians, successful against Jellachich, drove him upon Vienna, and by their victory strengthened the force that was to attack that town. Under these circumstances it was the clear duty of Hungary to support, without delay, and with all disposable forces, not the Diet of Vienna, not the Committee of Safety or any other official body at Vienna, but the *Viennese Revolution*. And if Hungary should even have forgotten that Vienna had fought the first battle of Hungary, she owed it to her own safety not to forget that Vienna was the only outpost of Hungarian independence, and that after the fall of Vienna nothing could meet the advance of the Imperial troops against herself. Now, we know very well all the Hungarians can say and have said in defence of their inactivity during the blockade and storming of Vienna: the insufficient state of their own force, the refusal of the Diet or any other official body in Vienna to call them in, the necessity to keep on constitutional ground, and to avoid complications with the German Central power. But the fact is, as to the insufficient state of the Hungarian army, that in the first days after the Viennese Revolution and the arrival of Jellachich, nothing was wanted in the shape of regular troops, as the Austrian regulars were very far from being concentrated; and that a courageous, unrelenting following up of the first advantage over Jellachich, even with nothing but the *Land Sturm* that had fought at Stuhlweissenburg, would have sufficed to effect a junction with the Viennese, and to adjourn to that day six months every concentration of an Austrian army. In war, and particularly in revolutionary warfare, rapidity of action until some decided advantage is gained is the first rule, and we have no hesitation in saying that upon *merely military grounds*, Perczel ought not to have stopped until his junction with the Viennese was effected. There was certainly some risk, but who ever won a battle without risking something? And did the people of Vienna risk nothing when they drew upon themselves—they, a population of four hundred thousand—the forces that were to march to the conquest of twelve millions of Hungarians? The military fault committed by waiting until the Austrians had united, and by making the feeble demonstration at Schwechat which ended, as it deserved to do, in an inglorious defeat—this military fault certainly incurred more risks than a resolute march upon Vienna against the disbanded brigands of Jellachich would have done.

But, it is said, such an advance of the Hungarians, unless authorised by some official body, would have been a violation of the German territory, would have brought on complications with the Central Power at Frankfort, and would have been, above all, an abandonment of the legal and constitutional policy which formed the strength of the Hungarian cause. Why, the official bodies in Vienna were nonentities! Was it the Diet, was it the popular Committees, who had risen for Hungary, or was it the people of Vienna, and they alone, who had taken to the musket to stand the brunt of the first battle for Hungary's independence? It was not this nor that official body in Vienna which it was important to uphold; all these bodies might, and would have been, upset very soon in the progress of the revolutionary development; but it was the ascendancy of the revolutionary movement, the unbroken progress of popular action itself, which alone was in question, and which alone could save Hungary from invasion. What forms this revolutionary movement afterwards might take, was the business of the Viennese, not of the Hungarians, so long as Vienna and German Austria at large continued their allies against the common enemy. But the question is, whether in this stickling of the Hungarian Government for some quasi-legal authorisation, we are not to see the first clear symptom of that pretence to a rather doubtful legality of proceeding, which, if it did not save Hungary, at least told very well, at a later period, before the English middle-class audiences.

As to the pretext of possible conflicts with the Central Power of Germany at Frankfort, it is quite futile. The Frankfort authorities were *de facto* upset by the victory of the Counter-Revolution at Vienna; they would have been equally upset had the Revolution there found the support necessary to defeat its enemies. And lastly, the great argument that Hungary could not leave legal and constitutional ground, may do very well for British free-traders, but it will never be deemed sufficient in the eyes of history. Suppose the people of Vienna had stuck to "legal and constitutional means" on March 13th, and on

GERMANY

October 6th, what then of the "legal and constitutional" movement, and of all the glorious battles which, for the first time, brought Hungary to the notice of the civilised world? The very legal and constitutional ground upon which it is asserted the Hungarians moved in 1848 and 1849 was conquered for them by the exceedingly illegal and unconstitutional rising of the people of Vienna on March 13th. It is not to our purpose here to discuss the revolutionary history of Hungary, but it may be deemed proper if we observe that it is utterly useless to professedly use merely legal means of resistance against an enemy who scorns such scruples; and if we add, that had it not been for this eternal pretence of legality which Görgey seized upon and turned against the Government, the devotion of Görgey's army to its general, and the disgraceful catastrophe of Villagos, would have been impossible. And when, at last, to save their honour, the Hungarians came across the Leitha, in the latter end of October 1848, was not this quite as illegal as any immediate and resolute attack would have been?

We are known to harbour no unfriendly feeling toward Hungary. We stood by her during the struggles; we may be allowed to say that our paper, the *Neue Rheinische Zeitung*, has done more than any other to render the Hungarian cause popular in Germany, by explaining the nature of the struggle between the Magyar and Slavonian races, and by following up the Hungarian war in a series of articles which have had paid them the compliment of being plagiarised in almost every subsequent book upon the subject, the works of native Hungarians and "eye-witnesses" not excepted. We even now, in any future continental convulsion, consider Hungary as the necessary and natural ally of Germany. But we have been severe enough upon our own countrymen, to have a right to speak out upon our neighbours; and then we have here to record facts with historical impartiality, and we must say that in this particular instance, the generous bravery of the people of Vienna was not only far more noble, but also more far-sighted than the cautious circumspection of the Hungarian Government. And, as a German, we may further be allowed to say, that not for all the showy victories and glorious battles of the Hungarian campaign, would we exchange that spontaneous, single-handed rising, and heroic resistance of the people of Vienna, our countrymen, which gave

Hungary the time to organise the army that could do such great things.

The second ally of Vienna was the German people. But they were everywhere engaged in the same struggle as the Viennese. Frankfort, Baden, Cologne, had just been defeated and disarmed. In Berlin and Breslau the people were at daggers drawn with the army, and daily expected to come to blows. Thus it was in every local centre of action. Everywhere questions were pending that could only be settled by the force of arms; and now it was that for the first time were severely felt the disastrous consequences of the continuation of the old dismemberment and decentralisation of Germany. The different questions in every State, every province, every town, were fundamentally the same; but they were brought forward everywhere under different shapes and pretexts, and had everywhere attained different degrees of maturity. Thus it happened that while in every locality the decisive gravity of the events at Vienna was felt, yet nowhere could an important blow be struck with any hope of bringing the Viennese succour, or making a diversion in their favour; and there remained nothing to aid them but the Parliament and Central Power of Frankfort; they were appealed to on all hands; but what did they do?

The Frankfort Parliament and the bastard child it had brought to light by incestuous intercourse with the old German Diet, the so-called Central Power, profited by the Viennese movement to show forth their utter nullity. This contemptible Assembly, as we have seen, had long since sacrificed its virginity, and young as it was, it was already turning grey-headed and experienced in all the artifices of prating and pseudo-diplomatic prostitution. Of the dreams and illusions of power, of German regeneration and unity, that in the beginning had pervaded it, nothing remained but a set of Teutonic claptrap phraseology, that was repeated on every occasion, and a firm belief of each individual member in his own importance, as well as in the credulity of the public. The original naïveté was discarded; the representatives of the German people had turned practical men, that is to say, they had made it out that the less they did, and the more they prated, the safer would be their position as the umpires of the fate of Germany. Not that they considered their proceedings superfluous; quite the contrary. But they had found out that all really great questions, being to them forbidden ground, had better be let alone, and there, like a set of Byzantine doctors of the Lower Empire, they discussed with an importance and assiduity worthy of the fate that at last overtook them, theoretical dogmas long ago settled in every part of the civilised world, or microscopical practical questions which never led to any practical result. Thus, the Assembly being a sort of Lancastrian School for the mutual instruction of members, and being, therefore, very important to themselves, they were persuaded it was doing even more than the German people had a right to expect, and looked upon everyone as a traitor to the country who had the impudence to ask them to come to any result.

When the Viennese insurrection broke out, there was a host of interpellations, debates, motions, and amendments upon it, which, of course, led to nothing. The Central Power was to interfere. It sent two commissioners, Welcker, the ex-Liberal, and Mosle, to Vienna. The travels of Don Quixote and Sancho Panza form matter for an Odyssey in comparison with the heroic feats and wonderful adventures of those two knight-errants of German Unity. Not daring to go to Vienna, they were bullied by Windischgrätz, wondered at by the idiot Emperor, and impudently hoaxed by the Minister Stadion. Their despatches and reports are perhaps the only portion of the Frankfort transactions that will retain a place in German literature; they are a perfect satirical romance, ready cut and dried, and an eternal monument of disgrace for the Frankfort Assembly and its Government.

The left side of the Assembly had also sent two commissioners to Vienna, in order to uphold its authority there—Froebel and Robert Blum. Blum, when danger drew near, judged rightly that here the great battle of the German Revolution was to be fought, and unhesitatingly resolved to stake his head on the issue. Froebel, on the contrary, was of opinion that it was his duty to preserve himself for the important duties of his post at Frankfort. Blum was considered one of the most eloquent men of the Frankfort Assembly; he certainly was the most popular. His eloquence would not have stood the test of any experienced Parliamentary Assembly; he was too fond of the shallow declamtions of a German dissenting preacher, and his arguments wanted both philosophical acumen and acquaintance with practical matters of fact. In politics he belonged to "Moderate Democracy," a rather indefinite sort of thing, cherished on account of this very want of definiteness in its principles. But with all this Robert Blum was by nature a thorough, though somewhat polished, plebeian, and in decisive moments his plebeian instinct and plebeian energy got the better of his indefiniteness, and, therefore, indecisive political persuasion and knowledge. In such moments he raised himself far above the usual standard of his capacities.

Thus, in Vienna, he saw at a glance that here, not in the midst of the would-be elegant debates of Frankfort, the fate of his country would have to be decided. He at once made up his mind, gave up all idea of retreat, took a command in the revolutionary force, and behaved with extraordinary coolness and decision. It was he who retarded for a considerable time the taking of the town, and covered one of its sides from attack by burning the Tabor Bridge over the Danube. Everybody knows how, after the storming, he was arrested, tried by court-martial, and shot. He died like a hero. And the Frankfort Assembly, horrorstruck as it was, yet took the bloody insult with a seeming good grace. A resolution was carried, which, by the softness and diplomatic decency of its language, was more an insult to the grave of the murdered martyr than a damning stain upon Austria. But it was not to be expected that this contemptible Assembly should resent the assassination of one of its members, particularly of the leader of the Left.

New York Daily Tribune, April 9th, 1852.

XIII

London, March 1852.

ON November 1st Vienna fell, and on the 9th of the same month the dissolution of the Constituent Assembly in Berlin showed how much this event had at once raised the spirit and the strength of the Counter-Revolutionary party all over Germany.

The events of the summer of 1848 in Prussia are soon told. The Constituent Assembly, or rather " the Assembly elected for the purpose of agreeing upon a Constitution with the Crown," and its majority of representatives of the middle-class interest, had long since forfeited all public esteem by lending itself to the intrigues of the Court, from fear of the more energetic elements of the population. They had confirmed, or rather restored, the obnoxious privileges of feudalism, and thus betrayed the liberty and the interests of the peasantry. They had neither been able to draw up a Constitution, nor to amend in any way the general legislation. They had occupied themselves almost exclusively with nice theoretical distinctions, mere formalities, and questions of constitutional etiquette. The Assembly, in fact, was more a school of Parliamentary *savoir vivre* for its members, than a body in which the people could take any interest. The majorities were, besides, very nicely balanced, and almost always decided by the wavering centres whose oscillations from right to left, and vice versa, upset, first the ministry of Camphausen, then that of Auerswald and Hansemann. But while thus the Liberals, here as everywhere else, let the occasion slip out of their hands, the Court reorganised its elements of strength among the nobility, and the most uncultivated portion of the rural population, as well as in the army and the bureaucracy. After Hansemann's downfall, a ministry of bureaucrats and military officers, all staunch reactionists, was formed, which, however, seemingly gave way to the demand of the Parliament; and the Assembly acting upon the commodious principle of " measures, not men," were actually duped into applauding this ministry, while they, of course, had no eyes for the concentration and organisation of Counter-Revolutionary forces, which that same ministry carried on pretty openly. At last, the signal being given by the fall of Vienna, the King dismissed its ministers, and replaced them by " men of action," under the leadership of the present premier, Manteufel. Then the dreaming Assembly at once awoke to the danger; it passed a vote of no confidence in the Cabinet, which was at once replied to by a decree removing the Assembly from Berlin, where it might, in case of a conflict, count upon the support of the masses, to Brandenburg, a petty provincial town dependent entirely upon the Government. The Assembly, however, declared that it could not be adjourned, removed, or dissolved, except with its own consent. In the meantime, General Wrangel entered Berlin at the head of some forty thousand troops. In a meeting of the municipal magistrates and the officers of the National Guard, it was resolved not to offer any resistance. And now, after the Assembly and its Constituents, the Liberal bourgeoisie, had allowed the combined reactionary party to occupy every important position, and to wrest from their hands almost every means of defence, began that grand comedy of " passive and legal resistance " which they intended to be a glorious imitation of the example of Hampden, and of the first efforts of the Americans in the War of Independence. Berlin was declared in a state of siege, and Berlin remained tranquil ; the National Guard was dissolved by the Government, and its arms were delivered up with the greatest punctuality. The Assembly was hunted down during a fortnight, from one place of meeting to another, and everywhere dispersed by the military, and the members of the Assembly begged of the citizens to remain tranquil. At last the Government having declared the Assembly dissolved, it passed a resolution to declare the levying of taxes illegal, and then its members dispersed themselves over the country to organise the refusal of taxes. But they found that they had been woefully mistaken in the choice of their means. After a few agitated weeks followed by severe measures of the Government against the Opposition, everyone gave up the idea of refusing the taxes in order to please a defunct Assembly that had not even had the courage to defend itself.

Whether it was in the beginning of November 1848, already too late to try armed resistance, or whether a part of the army, on finding serious opposition, would have turned over to the side of the Assembly, and thus decided the matter in its favour, is a question which may never be solved. But in revolution as in war, it is always necessary to show a strong front, and he who attacks is in the advantage; and in revolution as in war, it is of the highest necessity to stake everything on the decisive moment, whatever the odds may be. There is not a single successful revolution in history that does not prove the truth of these axioms. Now, for the Prussian Revolution, the decisive moment had come in November 1848; the Assembly, at the head, officially, of the whole revolutionary interest, did neither show a strong front, for it receded at every advance of the enemy; much less did it attack, for it chose even not to defend itself; and when the decisive moment came, when Wrangel, at the head of forty thousand men, knocked at the gates of Berlin, instead of finding as he and all his officers fully expected, every street studded with barricades, every window turned into a loop-hole, he found the gates open, and the streets obstructed only by peaceful Berliner burghers, enjoying the joke they had played upon him, by delivering themselves up, hands and feet tied, unto the astonished soldiers. It is true, the Assembly and the people, if they had resisted, might have been beaten; Berlin might have been bombarded, and many hundreds might have been killed, without preventing the ultimate victory of the Royalist party. But that was no reason why they should surrender their arms at once. A well-contested defeat is a fact of as much revolutionary importance as an easily-won victory. The defeats of Paris in June 1848 and of Vienna in October, certainly did far more in revolutionising the minds of the people of these two cities than the victories of February and March. The Assembly and the people of Berlin would, probably, have shared the fate of the two towns abovenamed; but they would have fallen gloriously, and would have left behind themselves, in the minds of the survivors, a wish of revenge, which in revolutionary times is one of the highest incentives to energetic and passionate action. It is a matter of course that, in every struggle, he who takes up the gauntlet risks being beaten; but is that a reason why he should confess himself beaten, and submit to the yoke without drawing the sword?

REVOLUTION AND COUNTER-REVOLUTION 83

In a revolution he who commands a decisive position and surrenders it, instead of forcing the enemy to try his hand at an assault, invariably deserves to be treated as a traitor.

The same decree of the King of Prussia which dissolved the Constituent Assembly also proclaimed a new Constitution, founded upon the draft which had been made by a Committee of that Assembly, but enlarging in some points the powers of the Crown, and rendering doubtful in others those of the Parliament. This Constitution established two Chambers, which were to meet soon for the purpose of confirming and revising it.

We need hardly ask where the German National Assembly was during the "legal and peaceful" struggle of the Prussian Constitutionalists. It was, as usual, at Frankfort, occupied with passing very tame resolutions against the proceedings of the Prussian Government, and admiring the "imposing spectacle of the passive, legal, and unanimous resistance of a whole people against brutal force." The Central Government sent commissioners to Berlin to intercede between the Ministry and the Assembly; but they met the same fate as their predecessors at Olmütz, and were politely shown out. The Left of the National Assembly, i.e., the so-called Radical party, sent also their commissioners; but after having duly convinced themselves of the utter helplessness of the Berlin Assembly, and confessed their own equal helplessness, they returned to Frankfort to report progress, and to testify to the admirably peaceful conduct of the population of Berlin. Nay, more; when Herr Bassermann, one of the Central Government's commissioners, reported that the late stringent measures of the Prussian ministers were not without foundation, inasmuch as there had of late been seen loitering about the streets of Berlin sundry savage-looking characters, such as always appear previous to anarchical movements (and which ever since have been named "Bassermannic characters"), these worthy deputies of the Left and energetic representatives of the revolutionary interest actually arose to make oath, and testify that such was not the case! Thus within two months the total impotency of the Frankfort Assembly was signally proved. There could be no more glaring proofs that this body was totally inadequate to its task; nay, that it had not even the remotest idea of what its task really was. The fact that both in Vienna and in Berlin the fate of the Revolution was settled, that in both these capitals the most important and vital questions were disposed of, without the existence of the Frankfort Assembly ever being taken the slightest notice of—this fact alone is sufficient to establish that the body in question was a mere debating-club, composed of a set of dupes, who allowed the Governments to use them as a Parliamentary puppet, shown to amuse the shopkeepers and petty tradesmen of petty States and petty towns, as long as it was considered convenient to divert the attention of these parties. How long this was considered convenient we shall soon see. But it is a fact worthy of attention that among all the " eminent " men of this Assembly there was not one who had the slightest apprehension of the part they were made to perform, and that even up to the present day ex-members of the Frankfort club have invariably organs of historical perception quite peculiar to themselves.

New York Daily Tribune, April 17th, 1852.

XIV

London, April 1852.

THE first months of the year 1849 were employed by the Austrian and Prussian Governments in following up the advantages obtained in October and November 1848. The Austrian Diet, ever since the taking of Vienna, had carried on a merely nominal existence in a small Moravian country town, named Kremsir. Here the Slavonian deputies, who, with their constituents, had been mainly instrumental in raising the Austrian Government from its prostration, were singularly punished for their treachery against the European Revolution. As soon as the Government had recovered its strength, it treated the Diet and its Slavonian majority with the utmost contempt, and when the first successes of the Imperial arms foreboded a speedy termination of the Hungarian War, the Diet, on March 4th, was dissolved, and the deputies dispersed by military force. Then at last the Slavonians saw that they were duped, and then they shouted: " Let us go to Frankfort and carry on there the opposition which we cannot pursue here! " But it was then too late, and the very fact that they had no other alternative than either to remain quiet or to join the impotent Frankfort Assembly, this fact alone was sufficient to show their utter helplessness.

Thus ended for the present, and most likely for ever, the attempts of the Slavonians of Germany to recover an independent national existence. Scattered remnants of numerous nations, whose nationality and political vitality had long been extinguished, and who in consequence had been obliged, for almost a thousand years, to follow in the wake of a mightier nation, their conqueror, the same as the Welsh in England, the Basques in Spain, the Bas-Bretons in France, and at a more recent period the Spanish and French Creoles in those portions of North America occupied of late by the Anglo-American race—these dying nationalities, the Bohemians, Carinthians, Dalmatians, etc., had tried to profit by the universal confusion of 1848, in order to restore their political *status quo* of A.D. 800. The history of a thousand years ought to have shown them that such a retrogression was impossible; that if all the territory east of the Elbe and Saale had at one time been occupied by kindred Slavonians, this fact merely proved the historical tendency, and at the same time physical and intellectual power of the German nation to subdue, absorb, and assimilate its ancient eastern neighbours; that this tendency of absorption on the part of the Germans had always been, and still was, one of the mightiest means by which the civilisation of Western Europe had been spread in the east of that continent; that it could only cease whenever the process of Germanisation had reached the frontier of large, compact, unbroken nations, capable of an independent national life, such as the Hungarians, and in some degree the Poles; and that, therefore, the natural and inevitable fate of these dying nations was to allow this process of dissolution and absorption by their stronger neighbours to complete itself. Certainly this is no very flattering prospect for the national ambition of the Panslavistic dreamers who succeeded in agitating a portion of the Bohemian and South Slavonian people; but can they expect that history would retrograde a thousand years in order to please a few phthisical bodies of men, who in every part of the territory they occupy are interspersed with and surrounded by Germans, who from time almost immemorial have had for all purposes of civilisation no other language but the German, and who lack the very first conditions of national existence, numbers and compactness of territory? Thus, the Panslavistic rising, which everywhere in the German and Hungarian Slavonic territories was the cloak for the restoration to independence of all these numberless petty nations, everywhere clashed with the European revolutionary movements, and the Slavonians, although pretending to fight for liberty, were invariably (the Democratic portion of the Poles excepted) found on the side of despotism and reaction. Thus it was in Germany, thus in Hungary, thus even here and there in Turkey. Traitors to the popular cause, supporters and chief props to the Austrian Government's cabal, they placed themselves in the position of outlaws in the eyes of all revolutionary nations. And although nowhere the mass of the people had a part in the petty squabbles about nationality raised by the

Panslavistic leaders, for the very reason that they were too ignorant, yet it will never be forgotten that in Prague, in a half-German town, crowds of Slavonian fanatics cheered and repeated the cry: "Rather the Russian knout than German Liberty!" After their first evaporated effort in 1848, and after the lesson the Austrian Government gave them, it is not likely that another attempt at a later opportunity will be made. But if they should try again under similar pretexts to ally themselves to the counter-revolutionary force, the duty of Germany is clear. No country in a state of revolution and involved in external war can tolerate a Vendée in its very heart.

As to the Constitution proclaimed by the Emperor at the same time with the dissolution of the Diet, there is no need to revert to it, as it never had a practical existence, and is now done away with altogether. Absolutism has been restored in Austria to all intents and purposes ever since March 4th, 1849.

In Prussia, the Chambers met in February for the ratification and revision of the new Charter proclaimed by the King. They sat for about six weeks, humble and meek enough in their behaviour toward the Government, yet not quite prepared to go the lengths the King and his ministers wished them to go. Therefore, as soon as a suitable occasion presented itself, they were dissolved.

Thus both Austria and Prussia had for the moment got rid of the shackles of parliamentary control. The Governments now concentrated all power in themselves, and could bring that power to bear wherever it was wanted: Austria upon Hungary and Italy, Prussia upon Germany. For Prussia, too, was preparing for a campaign by which "order" was to be restored in the smaller States.

Counter-revolution being now paramount in the two great centres of action in Germany,—in Vienna and Berlin,—there remained only the lesser States in which the struggle was still undecided, although the balance there, too, was leaning more and more against the revolutionary interest. These smaller States, we have said, found a common centre in the National Assembly at Frankfort. Now, this so-called National Assembly, although its reactionist spirit had long been evident, so much so that the very people of Frankfort had risen in arms against it, yet its origin was of a more or less revolutionary nature; it occupied an abnormal, revolutionary position in January; its competence had never been defined, and it had at last come to the decision—which, however, was never recognised by the larger States—that its resolutions had the force of law. Under these circumstances, and when the Constitutionalist-Monarchical party saw their positions turned by the recovering Absolutists, it is not to be wondered that the Liberal, monarchical bourgeoisie of almost the whole of Germany should place their last hopes upon the majority of this Assembly, just as the petty shopkeepers in the rest, the nucleus of the Democratic party, gathered in their growing distress around the minority of that same body, which indeed formed the last compact Parliamentary phalanx of Democracy. On the other hand, the larger Governments, and particularly the Prussian Ministry, saw more and more the incompatibility of such an irregular elective body with the restored monarchical system of Germany, and if they did not at once force its dissolution, it was only because the time had not yet come, and because Prussia hoped first to use it for the furthering of its own ambitious purposes.

In the meantime, that poor Assembly itself fell into a greater and greater confusion. Its deputations and commissaries had been treated with the utmost contempt, both in Vienna and Berlin; one of its members, in spite of his parliamentary inviolability, had been executed in Vienna as a common rebel. Its decrees were nowhere heeded; if they were noticed at all by the larger powers, it was merely by protesting notes which disputed the authority of the Assembly to pass laws and resolutions binding upon their Governments. The Representative of the Assembly, the Central Executive power, was involved in diplomatic squabbles with almost all the Cabinets of Germany, and, in spite of all their efforts, neither Assembly nor Central Government could bring Austria and Prussia to state their ultimate views, plans and demands. The Assembly, at last, commenced to see clearly, at least so far, that it had allowed all power to slip out of its hands, that it was at the mercy of Austria and Prussia, and that if it intended making a Federal Constitution for Germany at all, it must set about the thing at once and in good earnest. And many of the vacillating members also saw clearly that they had been egregiously duped by the Governments. But what were they, in their impotent position, able to do now?

The only thing that could have saved them would have been promptly and decidedly to pass over into the popular camp; but the success, even of that step, was more than doubtful; and then, where in this helpless crowd of undecided, short-sighted, self-conceited beings, who, when the eternal noise of contradictory rumours and diplomatic notes completely stunned them, sought their only consolation and support in the everlastingly repeated assurance that they were the best, the greatest, the wisest men of the country, and that they alone could save Germany—where, we say, among these poor creatures, whom a single year of Parliamentary life had turned into complete idiots, where were the men for a prompt and decisive resolution, much less for energetic and consistent action?

At last the Austrian Government threw off the mask. In its Constitution of March 4th, it proclaimed Austria an indivisible monarchy, with common finances, system of customs-duties, of military establishments, thereby effacing every barrier and distinction between the German and non-German provinces. This declaration was made in the face of resolutions and articles of the intended Federal Constitution which had been already passed by the Frankfort Assembly. It was the gauntlet of war thrown down to it by Austria, and the poor Assembly had no other choice but to take it up. This it did with a deal of blustering, which Austria, in the consciousness of her power, and of the utter nothingness of the Assembly, could well afford to allow to pass. And this precious representation, as it styled itself, of the German people, in order to revenge itself for this insult on the part of Austria, saw nothing better before it than to throw itself, hands and feet tied, at the feet of the Prussian Government. Incredible as it would seem, it bent its knees before the very ministers whom it had condemned as unconstitutional and antipopular, and whose dismissal it had in vain insisted upon. The details of this disgraceful transaction, and the tragi-comical events that followed, will form the subject of our next.

New York Daily Tribune, April 24th, 1852.

XV

London, July 1852.

WE now come to the last chapter in the history of the German Revolution; the conflict of the National Assembly with the Governments of the different States, especially of Prussia; the insurrection of Southern and Western Germany, and its final overthrow by Prussia.

We have already seen the Frankfort National Assembly at work. We have seen it kicked by Austria, insulted by Prussia, disobeyed by the lesser States, duped by its own impotent Central " Government," which again was the dupe of all and every prince in the country. But at last things began to look threatening for this weak, vacillating, insipid legislative body. It was forced to come to the conclusion that " the sublime idea of German unity was threatened in its realisation," which meant neither more nor less than that the Frankfort Assembly and all it had done, and was about to do, were very likely to end in smoke. Thus it set to work in good earnest in order to bring forth, as soon as possible, its grand production, the " Imperial Constitution." There was, however, one difficulty. What Executive Government was there to be ? An Executive Council ? No; that would have been, they thought in their wisdom, making Germany a Republic. A " president " ? That would come to the same. Thus they must revive the old Imperial dignity. But—as of course, a prince was to be emperor—who should it be ? Certainly none of the *Dei minorum gentium*, from Reuss-Schleitz-Greitz-Lobenstein-Ebersdorf up to Bavaria; neither Austria nor Prussia would have borne that. It could only be Austria or Prussia. But which of the two ? There is no doubt that, under otherwise favourable circumstances, this august Assembly would be sitting up to the present day, discussing this important dilemma without being able to come to a conclusion, if the Austrian Government had not cut the Gordian knot, and saved them the trouble.

Austria knew very well that from the moment in which she could again appear before Europe with all her provinces subdued, as a strong and great European power, the very law of political gravitation would draw the remainder of Germany into her orbit, without the help of any authority which an Imperial crown, conferred by the Frankfort Assembly, could give her. Austria had been far stronger, far freer in her movements, since she shook off the powerless crown of the German Empire—a crown which clogged her own independent policy, while it added not one iota to her strength, either within or without Germany. And supposing the case that Austria could not maintain her footing in Italy and Hungary, why, then she was dissolved, annihilated in Germany too, and could never pretend to re-seize a crown which had slipped from her hands while she was in the full possession of her strength. Thus Austria at once declared against all imperialist resurrections, and plainly demanded the restoration of the German Diet, the only Central Government of Germany known and recognised by the treaties of 1815; and on March 4th, 1849, issued that Constitution which had no other meaning than to declare Austria an indivisible, centralised, and independent monarchy, distinct even from that Germany which the Frankfort Assembly was to reorganise.

This open declaration of war left, indeed, the Frankfort wise-acres no other choice but to exclude Austria from Germany, and to create out of the remainder of that country a sort of lower empire, a " little Germany," the rather shabby Imperial mantle of which was to fall on the shoulders of His Majesty of Prussia. This, it will be recollected, was the renewal of an old project fostered some six or eight years ago by a party of South and Middle German Liberal doctrinaires, who considered as a god-send the degrading circumstances by which their old crotchet was now again brought forward as the latest " new move " for the salvation of the country.

They accordingly finished, in February and March 1849, the debate on the Imperial Constitution, together with the Declaration of Rights and the Imperial Electoral Law; not, however, without being obliged to make, in a great many points, the most contradictory concessions—now to the Conservative or rather Reactionary party—now to the more advanced factions of the Assembly. In fact, it was evident that the leadership of the

Assembly, which had formerly belonged to the Right and Right Centre (the Conservatives and Reactionists), was gradually, although slowly, passing toward the Left or Democratic side of that body. The rather dubious position of the Austrian deputies in an Assembly which had excluded their country from Germany, and in which they yet were called upon to sit and vote, favoured the derangement of its equipoise; and thus, as early as the end of February, the Left Centre and Left found themselves, by the help of the Austrian votes, very generally in a majority, while on other days the Conservative faction of the Austrians, all of a sudden, and for the fun of the thing, voting with the Right, threw the balance again on the other side. They intended, by these sudden *soubresauts*, to bring the Assembly into contempt, which, however, was quite unnecessary, the mass of the people being long since convinced of the utter hollowness and futility of anything coming from Frankfort. What a specimen of a Constitution, in the meantime, was framed under such jumping and counter-jumping, may easily be imagined.

The Left of the Assembly—this *élite* and pride of revolutionary Germany, as it believed itself to be—was entirely intoxicated with the few paltry successes it obtained by the goodwill, or rather the ill will, of a set of Austrian politicians, acting under the instigation and for the interest of Austrian despotism. Whenever the slightest approximation to their own not very well-defined principles had, in a homœopathically diluted shape, obtained a sort of sanction by the Frankfort Assembly, these Democrats proclaimed that they had saved the country and the people. These poor, weak-minded men, during the course of their generally very obscure lives, had been so little accustomed to anything like success, that they actually believed their paltry amendments, passed with two or three votes majority, would change the face of Europe. They had, from the beginning of their legislative career, been more imbued than any other faction of the Assembly with that incurable malady *Parliamentary crétinism*, a disorder which penetrates its unfortunate victims with the solemn conviction that the whole world, its history and future, are governed and determined by a majority of votes in that particular representative body which has the honour to count them among its members, and that all and everything going on outside the walls of their house—wars, revolutions, railway-constructing, colonising of whole new continents, California gold discoveries, Central American canals, Russian armies, and whatever else may have some little claim to influence upon the destinies of mankind—is nothing compared with the incommensurable events hinging upon the important question, whatever it may be, just at that moment occupying the attention of their honourable house. Thus it was the Democratic party of the Assembly, by effectually smuggling a few of their nostrums into the " Imperial Constitution," first became bound to support it, although in every essential point it flatly contradicted their own oft-proclaimed principles, and at last, when this mongrel work was abandoned, and bequeathed to them by its main authors, accepted the inheritance, and held out for this *Monarchical* Constitution, even in opposition to everybody who *then* proclaimed their own *Republican* principles.

But it must be confessed that in this the contradiction was merely apparent. The indeterminate, self-contradictory, immature character of the Imperial Constitution was the very image of the immature, confused, conflicting political ideas of these Democratic gentlemen. And if their own sayings and writings—as far as they could write—were not sufficient proof of this, their action would furnish such proof; for among sensible people it is a matter of course to judge of a man, not by his professions, but by his actions; not by what he pretends to be, but by what he does, and what he really is; and the deeds of these heroes of German Democracy speak loud enough for themselves, as we shall learn by and by. However, the Imperial Constitution, with all its appendages and paraphernalia, was definitely passed, and on March 28th, the King of Prussia was, by 290 votes against 248 who abstained, and 200 who were absent, elected Emperor of Germany *minus* Austria. The historical irony was complete; the Imperial farce executed in the streets of astonished Berlin, three days after the Revolution of March 18th, 1848, by Frederick William IV, while in a state which elsewhere would come under the Maine Liquor Law—this disgusting farce, just one year afterwards, had been sanctioned by the pretended Representative Assembly of all Germany. That, then, was the result of the German Revolution!

New York Daily Tribune, July 27th, 1852.

XVI

London, July 1852.

The National Assembly of Frankfort, after having elected the King of Prussia Emperor of Germany (*minus* Austria), sent a deputation to Berlin to offer him the crown, and then adjourned. On April 3rd, Frederick William received the deputies. He told them that, although he accepted the right of precedence over all the other princes of Germany, which this vote of the people's representatives had given him, yet he could not accept the Imperial crown as long as he was not sure that the remaining princes acknowledged his supremacy, and the Imperial Constitution conferring those rights upon him. It would be, he added, for the Governments of Germany to see whether this Constitution was such as could be ratified by them. At all events, Emperor or not, he always would be found ready, he concluded, to draw the sword against either the external or the internal foe. We shall see how he kept his promise in a manner rather startling for the National Assembly.

The Frankfort wiseacres, after profound diplomatic inquiry, at last came to the conclusion that this answer amounted to a refusal of the crown. They then (April 12th) resolved: That the Imperial Constitution was the law of the land, and must be maintained; and not seeing their way at all before them, elected a Committee of thirty, to make proposals as to the means how this Constitution could be carried out.

This resolution was the signal for the conflict between the Frankfort Assembly and the German Governments which now broke out. The middle classes, and especially the smaller trading class, had all at once declared for the new Frankfort Constitution. They could not await any longer the moment which was " to close the Revolution." In Austria and Prussia the Revolution had, for the moment, been closed by the interference of the armed power. The classes in question would have preferred a less forcible mode of performing that operation, but they had not had a chance; the thing was done, and they had to make the best of it, a resolution which they at once took and carried out most heroically. In the smaller States, where things had been going on comparatively smoothly, the middle classes had long since been thrown back into that showy, but resultless, because powerless, parliamentary agitation, which was most congenial to themselves. The different States of Germany, as regarded each of them separately, appeared thus to have attained that new and definite form which was supposed to enable them to enter henceforth the path of peaceful constitutional development. There only remained one open question, that of the new political organisation of the German Confederacy. And this question, the only one which still appeared fraught with danger, it was considered a necessity to resolve at once. Hence the pressure exerted upon the Frankfort Assembly by the middle classes, in order to induce it to get the Constitution ready as soon as possible; hence the resolution among the higher and lower bourgeoisie to accept and support this Constitution, whatever it might be, in order to create a settled state of things without delay. Thus from the very beginning the agitation for the Imperial Constitution arose out of a reactionary feeling, and sprang up among these classes which were long since tired of the Revolution.

But there was another feature in it. The first and fundamental principles of the future German Constitution had been voted during the first months of spring and summer, 1848, a time when popular agitation was still rife. The resolutions then passed, though completely reactionary *then*, now, after the arbitrary acts of the Austrian and Prussian Governments, appeared exceedingly Liberal, and even Democratic. The standard of comparison had changed. The Frankfort Assembly could not, without moral suicide, strike out these once-voted provisions, and model the Imperial Constitution upon those which the Austrian and Prussian Governments had dictated, sword in hand. Besides, as we have seen, the majority in that Assembly had changed sides, and the Liberal and Democratic party were rising in influence. Thus the Imperial Constitution not only was distinguished by its apparently exclusive popular origin, but at the same time, full of contradiction as it was, it yet was the most Liberal Constitution

G

in all Germany. Its greatest fault was, that it was a mere sheet of paper, with no power to back its provisions.

Under these circumstances it was natural that the so-called Democratic party, that is, the mass of the petty trading class, should cling to the Imperial Constitution. This class had always been more forward in its demands than the Liberal-Monarchico-Constitutional bourgeoisie; it had shown a bolder front, it had very often threatened armed resistance, it was lavish in its promises to sacrifice its blood and its existence in the struggle for freedom; but it had already given plenty of proofs that on the day of danger it was nowhere, and that it never felt more comfortable than the day after a decisive defeat, when everything being lost, it had at least the consolation to know that somehow or other the matter *was* settled. While, therefore, the adhesion of the large bankers, manufacturers, and merchants was of a more reserved character, more like a simple demonstration in favour of the Frankfort Constitution, the class just beneath them, our valiant Democratic shopkeepers, came forward in grand style, and, as usual, proclaimed they would rather spill their last drop of blood than let the Imperial Constitution fall to the ground.

Supported by these two parties, the bourgeois adherents of the Constitutional Royalty, and the more or less Democratic shopkeepers, the agitation for the immediate establishment of the Imperial Constitution gained ground rapidly, and found its most powerful expression in the Parliaments of the several States. The Chambers of Prussia, of Hanover, of Saxony, of Baden, of Würtemburg, declared in its favour. The struggle between the Governments and the Frankfort Assembly assumed a threatening aspect.

The Governments, however, acted rapidly. The Prussian Chambers were dissolved, anti-constitutionally, as they had to revise and confirm the Constitution; riots broke out at Berlin, provoked intentionally by the Government, and the next day, April 28th, the Prussian Ministry issued a circular note, in which the Imperial Constitution was held up as a most anarchical and revolutionary document, which it was for the Governments of Germany to remodel and purify. Thus Prussia denied, point-blank, that sovereign constituent power which the wise men at Frankfort had always boasted of, but never established. Thus a

Congress of Princes, a renewal of the old Federal Diet, was called upon to sit in judgment on that Constitution which had already been promulgated as law. And at the same time Prussia concentrated troops at Kreuznach, three days' march from Frankfort, and called upon the smaller States to follow its example, by also dissolving their Chambers as soon as they should give their adhesion to the Frankfort Assembly. This example was speedily followed by Hanover and Saxony.

It was evident that a decision of the struggle by force of arms could not be avoided. The hostility of the Governments, the agitation among the people, were daily showing themselves in stronger colours. The military were everywhere worked upon by the Democratic citizens, and in the south of Germany with great success. Large mass meetings were everywhere held, passing resolutions to support the Imperial Constitution and the National Assembly, if need should be, with force of arms. At Cologne, a meeting of deputies of all the municipal councils of Rhenish Prussia took place for the same purpose. In the Palatinate, at Bergen, Fulda, Nuremberg, in the Odenwald, the peasantry met by myriads and worked themselves up into enthusiasm. At the same time the Constituent Assembly of France dissolved, and the new elections were prepared amid violent agitation, while on the eastern frontier of Germany, the Hungarians had within a month, by a succession of brilliant victories, rolled back the tide of Austrian invasion from the Theiss to the Leitha, and were every day expected to take Vienna by storm. Thus, popular imagination being on all hands worked up to the highest pitch, and the aggressive policy of the Governments defining itself more clearly every day, a violent collision could not be avoided, and cowardly imbecility only could persuade itself that the struggle was to come off peaceably. But this cowardly imbecility was most extensively represented in the Frankfort Assembly.

New York Daily Tribune, August 19th, 1852.

XVII

London, August 1852.

THE inevitable conflict between the National Assembly of Frankfort and the States Governments of Germany at last broke out in open hostilities during the first days of May 1849. The Austrian deputies, recalled by their Government, had already left the Assembly and returned home, with the exception of a few members of the Left or Democratic party. The great body of the Conservative members, aware of the turn things were about to take, withdrew even before they were called upon to do so by their respective Governments. Thus, even independently of the causes which in the foregoing letters have been shown to strengthen the influence of the Left, the mere desertion of their posts by the members of the Right, sufficed to turn the old minority into a majority of the Assembly. The new majority, which, at no former time, had dreamt of ever obtaining that good fortune, had profited by their places on the opposition benches to spout against the weakness, the indecision, the indolence of the old majority, and of its Imperial Lieutenancy. Now all at once, *they* were called on to replace that old majority. *They* were now to show what they could perform. Of course, *their* career was to be one of energy, determination, activity. *They*, the *élite* of Germany, would soon be able to drive onwards the senile Lieutenant of the Empire, and his vacillating ministers, and in case that was impossible they would—there could be no doubt about it—by force of the sovereign right of the people, depose that impotent Government, and replace it by an energetic, indefatigable Executive, who would assure the salvation of Germany. Poor fellows! *Their* rule—if rule it can be named, where no one obeyed—was a still more ridiculous affair than even the rule of their predecessors.

The new majority declared that, in spite of all obstacles, the Imperial Constitution must be carried out, and *at once;* that on

98

July 15th ensuing, the people were to elect the deputies of the new House of Representatives, and that this House was to meet at Frankfort on August 15th following. Now, this was an open declaration of war against those Governments that had not recognised the Imperial Constitution, the foremost among which were Prussia, Austria, Bavaria, comprising more than three-fourths of the German population; a declaration of war which was speedily accepted by them. Prussia and Bavaria, too, recalled the deputies sent from their territories to Frankfort, and hastened their military preparations against the National Assembly, while, on the other hand, the demonstrations of the Democratic party (out of Parliament) in favour of the Imperial Constitution and of the National Assembly, acquired a more turbulent and violent character, and the mass of the working people, led by the men of the most extreme party, were ready to take up arms in a cause which, if it was not their own, at least gave them a chance of somewhat approaching their aims by clearing Germany of its old monarchical encumbrances. Thus everywhere the people and the Governments were at daggers drawn upon this subject; the outbreak was inevitable; the mine was charged, and it only wanted a spark to make it explode. The dissolution of the Chambers in Saxony, the calling in of the Landwehr (military reserve) in Prussia, the open resistance of the Government to the Imperial Constitution, were such sparks; they fell, and all at once the country was in a blaze. In Dresden, on May 4th, the people victoriously took possession of the town, and drove out the King, while all the surrounding districts sent reinforcements to the insurgents. In Rhenish Prussia and Westphalia the Landwehr refused to march, took possession of the arsenals, and armed itself in defence of the Imperial Constitution. In the Palatinate the people seized the Bavarian Government officials, and the public moneys, and instituted a Committee of Defence, which placed the province under the protection of the National Assembly. In Würtemberg the people forced the King to acknowledge the Imperial Constitution, and in Baden the army, united with the people, forced the Grand Duke to flight, and erected a Provincial Government. In other parts of Germany the people only awaited a decisive signal from the National Assembly to rise in arms and place themselves at its disposal.

GERMANY

The position of the National Assembly was far more favourable than could have been expected after its ignoble career. The western half of Germany had taken up arms in its behalf; the military everywhere were vacillating; in the lesser States they were undoubtedly favourable to the movement. Austria was prostrated by the victorious advance of the Hungarians, and Russia, that reserve force of the German Governments, was straining all its powers in order to support Austria against the Magyar armies. There was only Prussia to subdue, and with the revolutionary sympathies existing in that country, a chance certainly existed of attaining that end. Everything then depended upon the conduct of the Assembly.

Now, insurrection is an art quite as much as war or any other, and subject to certain rules of proceeding, which, when neglected, will produce the ruin of the party neglecting them. Those rules, logical deductions from the nature of the parties and the circumstances one has to deal with in such a case, are so plain and simple that the short experience of 1848 had made the Germans pretty well acquainted with them. Firstly, never play with insurrection unless you are fully prepared to face the consequences of your play. Insurrection is a calculus with very indefinite magnitudes the value of which may change every day; the forces opposed to you have all the advantage of organisation, discipline, and habitual authority; unless you bring strong odds against them you are defeated and ruined. Secondly, the insurrectionary career once entered upon, act with the greatest determination, and on the offensive. The defensive is the death of every armed rising; it is lost before it measures itself with its enemies. Surprise your antagonists while their forces are scattering, prepare new successes, however small, but daily; keep up the moral ascendancy which the first successful rising has given to you; rally those vacillating elements to your side which always follow the strongest impulse, and which always look out for the safer side; force your enemies to a retreat before they can collect their strength against you; in the words of Danton, the greatest master of revolutionary policy yet known, *de l'audace, de l'audace, encore de l'audace!*

What, then, was the National Assembly of Frankfort to do if it would escape the certain ruin which it was threatened with? First of all, to see clearly through the situation, and to convince itself that there was now no other choice than either to submit to the Governments unconditionally, or take up the cause of the armed insurrection without reserve or hesitation. Secondly, to publicly recognise all the insurrections that had already broken out, and to call the people to take up arms everywhere in defence of the national representation, outlawing all princes, ministers and others who should dare to oppose the sovereign people represented by its mandatories. Thirdly, to at once depose the German Imperial Lieutenant, to create a strong, active, unscrupulous Executive, to call insurgent troops to Frankfort for its immediate protection, thus offering at the same time a legal pretext for the spread of the insurrection, to organise into a compact body all the forces at its disposal, and, in short, to profit quickly and unhesitatingly by every available means for strengthening its position and impairing that of its opponents.

Of all this the virtuous Democrats in the Frankfort Assembly did just the contrary. Not content with letting things take the course they liked, these worthies went so far as to suppress by their opposition all insurrectionary movements which were preparing. Thus, for instance, did Herr Karl Vogt at Nuremberg. They allowed the insurrections of Saxony, of Rhenish Prussia, of Westphalia to be suppressed without any other help than a posthumous, sentimental protest against the unfeeling violence of the Prussian Government. They kept up an underhand diplomatic intercourse with the South German insurrections but never gave them the support of their open acknowledgment. They knew that the Lieutenant of the Empire sided with the Governments, and yet they called upon *him*, who never stirred, to oppose the intrigues of these Governments. The ministers of the Empire, old Conservatives, ridiculed this impotent Assembly in every sitting, and they suffered it. And when William Wolff, a Silesian deputy, and one of the editors of the *New Rhenish Gazette*, called upon them to outlaw the Lieutenant of the Empire—who was, he justly said, nothing but the first and greatest traitor to the Empire, he was hooted down by the unanimous and virtuous indignation of those Democratic Revolutionists! In short, they went on talking, protesting, proclaiming, pronouncing, but never had the courage or the sense to act; while the hostile troops of the Governments drew nearer and nearer, and their own Executive, the Lieutenant of the Empire, was busily plotting with the German princes their speedy destruction. Thus even the last vestige of consideration was lost to this contemptible Assembly; the insurgents who had risen to defend it ceased to care any more for it, and when at last it came to a shameful end, as we shall see, it died without anybody taking any notice of its unhonoured exit.

New York Daily Tribune, September 18th, 1852.

XVIII

London (undated).

In our last we showed that the struggle between the German Governments on the one side, and the Frankfort Parliament on the other, had ultimately acquired such a degree of violence that in the first days of May, a great portion of Germany broke out in open insurrection; first Dresden, then the Bavarian Palatinate, parts of Rhenish Prussia, and at last Baden.

In all cases, the *real fighting* body of the insurgents, that body which first took up arms and gave battle to the troops, consisted of the *working classes of the towns*. A portion of the poorer country population, labourers and petty farmers, generally joined them after the outbreak of the conflict. The greater number of the young men of all classes, below the capitalist class, were to be found, for a time at least, in the ranks of the insurgent armies, but this rather indiscriminate aggregate of young men very soon thinned as the aspect of affairs took a somewhat serious turn. The students particularly, those " representatives of intellect," as they liked to call themselves, were the first to quit their standards, unless they were retained by the bestowal of officer's rank, for which they, of course, had very seldom any qualifications.

The working class entered upon this insurrection as they would have done upon any other which promised either to remove some obstacles in their progress towards political dominion and social revolution, or, at least, to tie the more influential but less courageous classes of society to a more decided and revolutionary course than they had followed hitherto. The working class took up arms with a full knowledge that this was, in the direct bearings of the case, no quarrel of its own; but it followed up its only true policy, to allow no class that has risen on its shoulders (as the bourgeoisie had done in 1848) to fortify its class-government, without opening, at least, a fair field to the working classes for the struggle for its own interests, and, in any case, to bring matters to a crisis, by which either the nation was fairly and irresistibly launched in the revolutionary career, or else the *status quo* before the Revolution restored as nearly as possible, and, thereby, a new revolution rendered unavoidable. In both cases the working classes represented the real and well-understood interest of the nation at large, in hastening as much as possible that revolutionary course which for the old societies of civilised Europe has now become a historical necessity, before any of them can again aspire to a more quiet and regular development of their resources.

As to country people that joined the insurrection, they were principally thrown into the arms of the Revolutionary party, partly by the relatively enormous load of taxation, and partly of feudal burdens pressing upon them.

Without any initiative of their own, they formed the tail of the other classes engaged in the insurrection, wavering between the working men on the one side, and the petty trading class on the other. Their own private social position, in almost every case decided which way they turned; the agricultural labourer generally supported the city artisan; the small farmer was apt to go hand in hand with the small shopkeeper.

This class of petty tradesmen, the great importance and influence of which we have already several times adverted to, may be considered as the leading class of the insurrection of May 1849. There being, this time, none of the large towns of Germany among the centre of the movement, the petty trading class, which in middling and lesser towns always predominates, found the means of getting the direction of the movement into its hands. We have, moreover, seen that, in this struggle for the Imperial Constitution, and for the rights of the German Parliament, there were the interests of this peculiar class at stake. The Provisional Governments formed in all the insurgent districts represented in the majority of each of them this section of the people, and the length they went to may therefore be fairly taken as the measure of what the German petty bourgeoisie is capable of—capable, as we shall see, of nothing but ruining any movement that entrusts itself to its hands.

The petty bourgeoisie, great in boasting, is very impotent for action, and very shy in risking anything. The *mesquin* character of its commercial transactions and its credit operations is eminently apt to stamp its character with a want of energy and enterprise; it is, then, to be expected that similar qualities will mark its political career. Accordingly the petty bourgeoisie encouraged insurrection by big words, and great boasting as to what it was going to do; it was eager to seize upon power as soon as the insurrection, much against its will, had broken out; it used this power to no other purpose but to destroy the effects of the insurrection. Wherever an armed conflict had brought matters to a serious crisis, there the shopkeepers stood aghast at the dangerous situation created for them; aghast at the people who had taken their boasting appeals to arms in earnest; aghast at the power thus thrust into their own hands; aghast, above all, at the consequences for themselves, for their social positions, for their fortunes, of the policy in which they were forced to engage themselves. Were they not expected to risk " life and property," as they used to say, for the cause of the insurrection ? Were they not forced to take official positions in the insurrection, whereby, in the case of defeat, they risked the loss of their capital ? And in case of victory, were they not sure to be immediately turned out of office, and to see their entire policy subverted by the victorious proletarians who formed the main body of their fighting army ? Thus placed between opposing dangers which surrounded them on every side, the petty bourgeoisie knew not to turn its power to any other account than to let everything take its chance, whereby, of course, there was lost what little chance of success there might have been, and thus to ruin the insurrection altogether. Its policy, or rather want of policy, everywhere was the same, and, therefore, the insurrections of May 1849, in all parts of Germany, are all cut out to the same pattern.

In Dresden, the struggle was kept on for four days in the streets of the town. The shopkeepers of Dresden, the " communal guard," not only did not fight, but in many instances favoured the proceedings of the troops against the insurgents. These again consisted almost exclusively of working men from the surrounding manufacturing districts. They found an able and cool-headed commander in the Russian refugee Michael Bakunin, who afterwards was taken prisoner, and now is confined in the dungeons of Munkacs, Hungary. The intervention of numerous Prussian troops crushed this insurrection.

In Rhenish Prussia the actual fighting was of little importance. All the large towns being fortresses commanded by citadels, there could be only skirmishing on the part of the insurgents. As soon as a sufficient number of troops had been drawn together, there was an end to armed opposition.

In the Palatinate and Baden, on the contrary, a rich, fruitful province and an entire state fell into the hands of the insurrection. Money, arms, soldiers, warlike stores, everything was ready for use. The soldiers of the regular army themselves joined the insurgents; nay, in Baden, they were amongst the foremost of them. The insurrectionists in Saxony and Rhenish Prussia sacrificed themselves in order to gain time for the organisation of the South German movement. Never was there such a favourable position for a provincial and partial insurrection as this. A revolution was expected in Paris; the Hungarians were at the gates of Vienna; in all the central States of Germany, not only the people, but even the troops, were strongly in favour of the insurrection, and only wanted an opportunity to join it openly. And yet the movement, having once got into the hands of the petty bourgeoisie, was ruined from its very beginning. The petty-bourgeois rulers, particularly of Baden—Herr Brentano at the head of them—never forgot that by usurping the place and prerogatives of the " lawful " sovereign, the Grand Duke, they were committing high treason. They sat down in their ministerial arm-chairs with the consciousness of criminality in their hearts. What can you expect of such cowards? They not only abandoned the insurrection to its own uncentralised, and therefore ineffective, spontaneity, they actually did everything in their power to take the sting out of the movement, to unman, to destroy it. And they succeeded, thanks to the zealous support of that deep class of politicians, the " Democratic " heroes of the petty bourgeoisie, who actually thought they were " saving the country," while they allowed themselves to be led by their noses by a few men of a sharper cast, such as Brentano.

As to the fighting part of the business, never were military operations carried on in a more slovenly, more stolid way than under the Baden General-in-Chief Sigel, an ex-lieutenant of the regular army. Everything was got into confusion, every good opportunity was lost, every precious moment was loitered away with planning colossal, but impracticable projects, until, when

REVOLUTION AND COUNTER-REVOLUTION

at last the talented Pole Mieroslawski took up the command, the army was disorganised, beaten, dispirited, badly provided for, opposed to an enemy four times more numerous, and withal, he could do nothing more than fight, at Waghäusel, a glorious though unsuccessful battle, carry out a clever retreat, offer a last hopeless fight under the walls of Rastatt, and resign. As in every insurrectionary war where armies are mixed of well-drilled soldiers and raw levies, there was plenty of heroism, and plenty of unsoldierlike, often unconceivable panic, in the revolutionary army; but, imperfect as it could not but be, it had at least the satisfaction that four times its number were not considered sufficient to put it to the rout, and that a hundred thousand regular troops, in a campaign against twenty thousand insurgents, treated them, militarily, with as much respect as if they had had to fight the Old Guard of Napoleon.

In May the insurrection had broken out; by the middle of July 1849, it was entirely subdued, and the first German Revolution was closed.

New York Daily Tribune, October 2nd, 1852.

XIX

London, September 24th, 1852.

WHILE the south and west of Germany was in open insurrection, and while it took the Governments from the first opening of hostilities at Dresden to the capitulation of Rastatt, rather more then ten weeks, to stifle this final blazing up of the first German Revolution, the National Assembly disappeared from the political theatre without any notice being taken of its exit.

We left this august body at Frankfort, perplexed by the insolent attacks of the Governments upon its dignity, by the impotency and treacherous listlessness of the Central Power it had itself created, by the risings of the petty trading class for its defence, and of the working class for a more revolutionary ultimate end. Desolation and despair reigned supreme among its members; events had at once assumed such a definite and decisive shape that in a few days the illusions of these learned legislators as to their real power and influence were entirely broken down. The Conservatives, at the signal given by the Governments, had already retired from a body which, henceforth, could not exist any longer, except in defiance of the constituted authorities. The Liberals gave the matter up in utter discomfiture; they, too, threw up their commissions as representatives. Honourable gentlemen decamped by hundreds. From eight or nine hundred members the number had dwindled down so rapidly that now one hundred and fifty, and a few days after one hundred, were declared a quorum. And even these were difficult to muster, although the whole of the Democratic party remained.

The course to be followed by the remnants of a parliament was plain enough. They had only to take their stand openly and decidedly with the insurrection, to give it, thereby, whatever strength legality could confer upon it, while they themselves at once acquired an army for their own defence.

They had to summon the Central Power to stop all hostilities at once; and if, as could be foreseen, this power neither could nor would do so, to depose it at once and put another more energetic Government in its place. If insurgent troops could not be brought to Frankfort (which, in the beginning when the State Governments were little prepared and still hesitating, might have been easily done), then the Assembly could have adjourned at once to the very centre of the insurgent district. All this done at once, and resolutely, not later than the middle or end of May, might have opened chances both for the insurrection and for the National Assembly.

But such a determined course was not to be expected from the representatives of German shopocracy. These aspiring statesmen were not at all freed from their illusions. Those members who had lost their fatal belief in the strength and inviolability of the Parliament had already taken to their heels; the Democrats who remained, were not so easily induced to give up dreams of power and greatness which they had cherished for a twelvemonth. True to the course they had hitherto pursued, they shrank back from decisive action until every chance of success, nay, every chance to succumb, with at least the honours of war, had passed away. In order, then, to develop a fictitious, busy-body sort of activity, the sheer impotency of which, coupled with its high pretension, could not but excite pity and ridicule, they continued insinuating resolutions, addressed, and requests to an Imperial Lieutenant, who not even noticed them; to ministers who were in open league with the enemy. And when at last William Wolff, member for Striegan, one of the editors of the *New Rhenish Gazette*, the only really revolutionary man in the whole Assembly, told them that if they meant what they said, they had better give over talking, and declare the Imperial Lieutenant, the chief traitor to the country, an outlaw at once; then the entire compressed virtuous indignation of these parliamentary gentlemen burst out with an energy which they never found when the Government heaped insult after insult upon them.

Of course, for Wolff's proposition was the first sensible word spoken within the walls of St. Paul's Church; of course, for it was the very thing that was to be done, and such plain language going so direct to the purpose, could not but insult a set of sentimentalists, who were resolute in nothing but irresolution, and who, too cowardly to act, had once for all made up their minds that in doing nothing, they were doing exactly what was to be done. Every word which cleared up, like lightning, the infatuated, but intentional nebulosity of their minds, every hint that was adapted to lead them out of the labyrinth where they obstinated themselves to take up as lasting an abode as possible, every clear conception of matters as they actually stood, was, of course, a crime against the majesty of this Sovereign Assembly.

Shortly after the position of the honourable gentlemen in Frankfort became untenable, in spite of resolutions, appeals, interpellations, and proclamations, they retreated, but not into the insurgent districts; that would have been too resolute a step. They went to Stuttgart, where the Würtemberg Government kept up a sort of expectative neutrality. There, at last, they declared the Lieutenant of the Empire to have forfeited his power, and elected from their own body a Regency of five. This Regency at once proceeded to pass a Militia law, which was actually in all due force sent to all the Governments of Germany.

They, the very enemies of the Assembly, were ordered to levy forces in its defence! Then there was created—on paper, of course—an army for the defence of the National Assembly. Divisions, brigades, regiments, batteries, everything was regulated and ordained. Nothing was wanted but reality, for that army, of course, was never called into existence.

One last scheme offered itself to the General Assembly. The Democratic population from all parts of the country sent deputations to place itself at the disposal of the Parliament, and to urge it on to a decisive action. The people, knowing what the intentions of the Würtemberg Government were, implored the National Assembly to force that Government into an open and active participation with their insurgent neighbours. But no. The National Assembly, in going to Stuttgart, had delivered itself up to the tender mercies of the Würtemberg Government. The members knew it, and repressed the agitation among the people. They thus lost the last remnant of influence which they might yet have retained. They earned the contempt they deserved, and the Würtemberg Government, pressed by Prussia and the Imperial Lieutenant, put a stop to the Democratic farce by shutting up, on June 18th, 1849, the room where the Parliament met, and by ordering the members of the Regency to leave the country.

Next they went to Baden, into the camp of the insurrection; but there they were now useless. Nobody noticed them. The Regency, however, in the name of the Sovereign German people, continued to save the country by its exertions. It made an attempt to get recognised by foreign powers, by delivering *passports* to anybody who would accept them. It issued proclamations, and sent commissioners to insurge those very districts of Würtemberg whose active assistance it had refused when it was yet time; of course, without effect. We have now under our eye an original report, sent to the Regency by one of these commissioners, Herr Roesler (member for Oels), the contents of which are rather characteristic. It is dated, Stuttgart, June 30th, 1849. After describing the adventures of half a dozen of these commissioners in a resultless search for cash, he gives a series of excuses for not having yet gone to his post, and then delivers himself of a most weighty argument respecting possible differences between Prussia, Austria, Bavaria, and Würtemberg, with their possible consequences. After having fully considered this, he comes, however, to the conclusion that there is no more chance. Next, he proposes to establish relays of trustworthy men for the conveyance of intelligence, and a system of espionage as to the intentions of the Würtemberg Ministry and the movements of the troops. This letter never reached its address, for when it was written the " Regency " had already passed entirely into the " foreign department," viz., Switzerland; and while poor Herr Roesler troubled his head about the intentions of the formidable ministry of a sixth-rate kingdom, a hundred thousand Prussian, Bavarian, and Hessian soldiers had already settled the whole affair in the last battle under the walls of Rastatt.

Thus vanished the German Parliament, and with it the first and last creation of the Revolution. Its convocation had been the first evidence that there actually *had been* a revolution in January; and it existed as long as this, the first modern German Revolution, was not yet brought to a close. Chosen under the influence of the capitalist class by a dismembered, scattered, rural population, for the most part only awakening from the dumbness of feudalism, this Parliament served to bring in one body upon the political arena all the great popular names of 1820-48, and

H

then to utterly ruin them. All the celebrities of middle-class Liberalism were here collected. The bourgeoisie expected wonders; it earned shame for itself and its representatives. The industrial and commercial capitalist class were more severely defeated in Germany than in any other country; they were first worsted, broken, expelled from office in every individual State of Germany, and then put to rout, disgraced and hooted in the Central German Parliament. Political Liberalism, the rule of the bourgeoisie, be it under a Monarchical or Republican form of government, is forever impossible in Germany.

In the latter period of its existence, the German Parliament served to disgrace forever that section which had ever since March 1848 headed the official opposition, the Democrats representing the interests of the small trading, and partially of the farming class. That class was, in May and June 1849, given a chance to show its means of forming a stable Government in Germany. We have seen how it failed; not so much by adverse circumstances as by the actual and continued cowardice in all trying movements that had occurred since the outbreak of the revolution; by showing in politics the same short-sighted, pusillanimous, wavering spirit, which is characteristic of its commercial operations. In May 1849, it had, by this course, lost the confidence of the real fighting mass of all European insurrections, the working class. But yet, it had a fair chance. The German Parliament belonged to it, exclusively, after the Reactionists and Liberals had withdrawn. The rural population was in its favour. Two-thirds of the armies of the smaller States, one-third of the Prussian army, the majority of the Prussian Landwehr (reserve or militia), were ready to join it, if it only acted resolutely, and with that courage which is the result of a clear insight into the state of things. But the politicians who led on this class were not more clear-sighted than the host of petty tradesmen which followed them. They proved even to be more infatuated, more ardently attached to delusions voluntarily kept up, more credulous, more incapable of resolutely dealing with facts than the Liberals. Their political importance, too, is reduced below the freezing-point. But not having actually carried their commonplace principles into execution, they were, under *very* favourable circumstances, capable of a momentary resurrection, when this last hope was taken from them, just as it was taken from their colleagues of the " pure Democracy " in France by the *coup d'état* of Louis Bonaparte.

The defeat of the south-west German insurrection, and the dispersion of the German Parliament, bring the history of the first German insurrection to a close. We have now to cast a parting glance upon the victorious members of the counter-revolutionary alliance; we shall do this in our next letter.

New York Daily Tribune, October 23rd, 1852.

XX

THE LATE TRIAL AT COLOGNE

London, December 1st, 1852.

You will have ere this received by the European papers numerous reports of the Communist Monster Trial at Cologne, Prussia, and of its result. But as none of the reports is anything like a faithful statement of the facts, and as these facts throw a glaring light upon the political means by which the continent of Europe is kept in bondage, I consider it necessary to revert to this trial.

The Communist or Proletarian party, as well as other parties, had lost, by suppression of the rights of association and meeting the means of giving to itself a legal organisation on the Continent. Its leaders, besides, had been exiled from their countries. But no political party can exist without an organisation; and that organisation which both the Liberal bourgeois and the Democratic shopkeeping class were enabled more or less to supply by the social station, advantages, and long-established, everyday intercourse of their members, the proletarian class, without such social station and pecuniary means, was necessarily compelled to seek in secret association. Hence, both in France and Germany, sprung up those numerous secret Societies which have, ever since 1849, one after another, been discovered by the police, and prosecuted as conspiracies; but if many of them were really conspiracies, formed with the actual intention of upsetting the Government for the time being,—and he is a coward that under certain circumstances would not conspire, just as he is a fool who, under other circumstances, would do so;—there were some other Societies which were formed with a wider and more elevated purpose, which knew that the upsetting of an existing Government was but a passing stage in the great impending struggle, and which intended to keep together and to prepare the party, whose nucleus they formed, for the last decisive combat which must, one day or another, crush forever in Europe the domination, not of mere " tyrants," " despots " and " usurpers," but of a power far superior, and far more formidable than theirs; that of capital over labour.

The organisation of the advanced Communist party in Germany was of that kind. In accordance with the principles of the " Manifesto " (published in 1848), and with those explained in the series of articles on " Revolution and Counter-Revolution in Germany," published in the *New York Daily Tribune*, this party never imagined itself capable of producing, at any time and at its pleasure, that revolution which was to carry its ideas into practice. It studied the causes that had produced the revolutionary movements in 1848, and the causes that made them fail. Recognising the social anatgonism of classes at the bottom of all political struggles, it applied itself to the study of the conditions under which one class of society can and must be called on to represent the whole of the interests of a nation, and thus politically to rule over it. History showed to the Communist party how, after the landed aristocracy of the Middle Ages, the monied power of the first capitalists arose and seized the reins of Government; how the social influence and political rule of this financial section of capitalists was superseded by the rising strength since the introduction of steam, of the manufacturing capitalists, and how at the present moment two more classes claim their turn of domination, the petty trading class and the industrial working class. The practical revolutionary experience of 1848-9 confirmed the reasonings of theory, which led to the conclusion that the Democracy of the petty traders must first have its turn, before the Communist working class could hope to permanently establish itself in power and destroy that system of wage-slavery which keeps it under the yoke of the bourgeoisie. Thus the secret organisation of the Communists could not have the direct purpose of upsetting the present Governments of Germany. Being formed to upset not these, but the insurrectionary Government which is sooner or later to follow them, its members might, and certainly would, individually, lend an active hand to a revolutionary movement against the present *status quo* in its turn; but the preparation of such a movement, otherwise than by secret spreading of Communist opinions by the masses, could not be an object of the Association. So well was this foundation of the

Society understood by the majority of its members, that when the place-hunting ambition of some tried to turn it into a conspiracy for making an extempore revolution, they were speedily turned out.

Now according to no law upon the face of the earth, could such an Association be called a plot, a conspiracy for purposes of high treason. If it was a conspiracy, it was one against, not the existing Government, but its probable successors. And the Prussian Government was aware of it. That was the cause why the eleven defendants were kept in solitary confinement during eighteen months, spent, on the part of the authorities, in the strangest judicial feats. Imagine, that after eight months' detention, the prisoners were remanded for some months more, " there being no evidence of any crime against them" ! And when at last they were brought before a jury, there was not a single overt act of a treasonable nature proved against them. And yet they were convicted, and you will speedily see how.

One of the emissaries of the society was arrested in May 1851, and from documents found upon him, other arrests followed. A Prussian police officer, a certain Stieber, was immediately ordered to trace the ramifications, in London, of the pretended plot. He succeeded in obtaining some papers connected with the above-mentioned seceders from the society, who had, after being turned out, formed an actual conspiracy in Paris and London. These papers were obtained by a double crime. A man named Reuter was bribed to break open the writing-desk of the secretary of the Society, and steal the papers therefrom. But that was nothing yet. This theft led to the discovery and conviction of the so-called Franco-German plot, in Paris, but it gave no clue as to the great Communist Association. The Paris plot, we may as well here observe, was under the direction of a few ambitious imbeciles and political *chevaliers d'industrie* in London, and of a formerly convicted forger, then acting as a police spy in Paris; their dupes made up, by rabid declamations and bloodthirsty rantings, for the utter insignificance of their political existence.

The Prussian police, then, had to look out for fresh discoveries. They established a regular office of secret police at the Prussian Embassy in London. A police agent, Greif by name, held his odious vocation under the title of an attaché to the Embassy—a step which should suffice to put all Prussian embassies out of the pale of international law, and which even the Austrians have not yet dared to take. Under him worked a certain Fleury, a merchant in the city of London, a man of some fortune and rather respectably connected, one of those low creatures who do the basest actions from an innate inclination to infamy. Another agent was a commercial clerk named Hirsch, who, however, had already been denounced as a spy on his arrival. He introduced himself into the society of some German Communist refugees in London, and they, in order to obtain proofs of his real character, admitted him for a short time. The proofs of his connection with the police were very soon obtained, and Herr Hirsch, from that time, absented himself. Although, however, he thus resigned all opportunities of gaining the information he was paid to procure, he was not inactive. From his retreat in Kensington, where he never met one of the Communists in question, he manufactured every week pretended reports of pretended sittings of a pretended Central Committee of that very conspiracy which the Prussian police could not get hold of. The contents of these reports were of the most absurd nature; not a Christian name was correct, not a name correctly spelt, not a single individual made to speak as he would be likely to speak. His master, Fleury, assisted him in his forgery, and it is not yet proved that " Attaché " Greif can wash his hands of these infamous proceedings. The Prussian Government, incredible to say, took these silly fabrications for gospel truth, and you may imagine what a confusion such depositions created in the evidence brought before the jury. When the trial came on, Herr Stieber, the already mentioned police officer, got into the witness-box, swore to all these absurdities, and, with no little self-complacency, maintained that he had a secret agent in the very closest intimacy with those parties in London who were considered the prime movers in this awful conspiracy. This secret agent was very secret indeed, for he had hid his face for eight months in Kensington, for fear he might actually see one of the parties whose most secret thoughts, words and doings, he pretended to report week after week.

Messrs. Hirsch and Fleury, however, had another invention in store. They worked up the whole of the reports they had made into an " original minute book " of the sittings of the Secret Supreme Committee, whose existence was maintained by the

Prussian police; and Herr Stieber, finding that this book wondrously agreed with the reports already received from the same parties, at once laid it before the jury, declaring upon his oath that after serious examination, and according to his fullest conviction, that book was genuine. It was then that most of the absurdities reported by Hirsch were made public. You may imagine the surprise of the pretended members of that Secret Committee when they found things stated of them which they never knew before. Some who were baptised William were here christened Louis or Charles; others, at the time they were at the other end of England, were made to have pronounced speeches in London; others were reported to have read letters they never had received; they were made to have met regularly on a Thursday, when they used to have a convivial reunion, once a week, on Wednesdays; a working man, who could hardly write, figured as one of the takers of minutes, and signed as such; and they all of them were made to speak in a language which, if it may be that of Prussian police stations, was certainly not that of a reunion in which literary men, favourably known in their country, formed the majority. And, to crown the whole, a receipt was forged for a sum of money, pretended to have been paid by the fabricators to the pretended secretary of the fictitious Central Committee for this book; but the existence of this pretended secretary rested merely upon a hoax that some malicious Communist had played upon the unfortunate Hirsch.

This clumsy fabrication was too scandalous an affair not to produce the contrary of its intended effect. Although the London friends of the defendants were deprived of all means to bring the facts of the case before the jury—although the letters they sent to the counsel for the defence were suppressed in the post—although the documents and affidavits they succeeded in getting into the hands of these legal gentlemen were not admitted in evidence, yet the general indignation was such that even the public accusers, nay, even Herr Stieber—whose oath had been given as a guarantee for the authenticity of that book—were compelled to recognise it as a forgery.

This forgery, however, was not the only thing of the kind of which the police were guilty. Two or three more cases of the sort came out during the trial. The documents stolen by Reuter were interpolated by the police so as to disfigure their meaning. A paper, containing some rabid nonsense, was written in a handwriting imitating that of Dr. Marx, and for a time it was pretended that it had been written by him, until at last the prosecution was obliged to acknowledge the forgery. But for every police infamy that was proved as such, there were five or six fresh ones brought forward, which could not, at the moment, be unveiled, the defence being taken by surprise, the proofs having to be got from London, and every correspondence of the counsel for the defence with the London Communist refugees being in open court treated as complicity in the alleged plot!

That Greif and Fleury are what they are here represented to be had been stated by Herr Stieber himself, in his evidence; as to Hirsch, he has before a London magistrate confessed that he forged the " minute book," by order and with the assistance of Fleury, and then made his escape from this country in order to evade a criminal prosecution.

The Government could stand few such branding disclosures as came to light during the trial. It had a jury such as the Rhenish Provinces had not yet seen—six nobles, two Government officials. These were not the men to look closely into the confused mass of evidence heaped before them during six weeks, when they heard it continually dinned into their ears that the defendants were the chiefs of a dreadful Communist conspiracy, got up in order to subvert everything sacred—property, family, religion, order, government and law! And yet, had not the Government, at the same time, brought it to the knowledge of the privileged classes, that an acquittal in this trial would be the signal for the suppression of the jury; and that it would be taken as a direct political demonstration—as a proof of the middle-class Liberal Opposition being ready to unite even with the most extreme revolutionists—the verdict would have been an acquittal. As it was, the retroactive application of the new Prussian code enabled the Government to have seven prisoners convicted, while four merely were acquitted, and those convicted were sentenced to imprisonment varying from three to six years, as you have, doubtless, already stated at the time the news reached you.

New York Daily Tribune, December 22nd, 1852.

APPENDIX I

HISTORY OF THE COMMUNIST LEAGUE

By Friedrich Engels

In the year 1834, a group of German refugees in Paris founded a secret society known as the Exiles' League. The organisation was democratic and republican in spirit. During the year 1836, the extremists broke away and constituted themselves into the Federation of the Just, a body whose members were mainly proletarian. The parent organisation, to which only such sleepyheads as Jakobus Venedey remained faithful, soon fell into a profound slumber; by the year 1840, when the police routed out a few sections, it was the merest shadow of its former self. The Federation, however, developed quickly. Originally it was a German outlyer of French working-class communism which owed its theoretical opinions mainly to the Babouvist tradition, and which was taking definite shape and form about this time in Paris. Among these circles, community of goods was demanded as the natural outcome of " equality." The aims of the Federation of the Just were the same as those of other Parisian secret societies of the period. Its activities were about evenly divided between propaganda and conspiratorial work. Paris was still regarded as the focal point of revolutionary action, although the preparation of revolutionary upheavals in Germany, should occasion arise, was not excluded from the programme. Since, however, Paris was looked upon as the place where the decisive battle would occur, the Federation was in reality not much more than a German branch of the French secret societies, and in especial of the Société des Saisons which was under the leadership of Blanqui (1805-81) and Barbès (1809-70). Indeed, the Federation was in such close touch with the Société des Saisons that, when the French rose in revolt on May 12th, 1839, the

APPENDICES

members of the Federation of the Just fought shoulder to shoulder with their French brothers and together they all suffered a common defeat.

Karl Schapper and Heinrich Bauer were arrested. The government of Louis Philippe was content to expel them from France after they had undergone a lengthy imprisonment while awaiting trial. Both men came to London. Schapper had been a student of forestry at Giessen University, and had, in 1832, participated in Georg Büchner's (1813-57) conspiracy. On April 3rd, 1833, he took part in the storming of the police station in Frankfort-on-the-Main. After this exploit he went abroad and in February 1834 joined Mazzini's forces in Savoy. Built on a heroic scale, resolute and energetic by temperament, ever ready to risk life and limb, Schapper was the prototype of the professional revolutionist of the eighteen-thirties. His steady development from demagogue to communist proves that, though his mind was somewhat obtuse, he was nevertheless receptive of new ideas. Once convinced, he held tenaciously to his opinions, and precisely because of this his passion for the cause often overwhelmed his better judgment. After the event he was always ready to acknowledge himself in the wrong. He was a man of genuine metal all through, and his services to the German working-class movement will never be forgotten.

Heinrich Bauer came from Franconia. He was a shoe-maker by trade, a little man of lively humour, alert and active. His diminutive frame held a fund of shrewdness and determination.

Once established in London, Schapper, who had been earning his living as compositor in Paris, now tried to blossom out as a teacher of languages. He and Bauer gathered up the broken threads of the Federation and made London the centre of its activities. Joseph Moll (died 1849) joined their company (he may already have done so in Paris). His trade was that of watchmaker; he came from Cologne; was a Hercules of moderate stature—how often have I seen him and Schapper triumphantly defend the entrance to a hall against hundreds of assailants!—; a man no less energetic and resolute than his two comrades, but far outstripping them in intelligence. Not only was he a born diplomatist, as the success of his innumerable missions amply testifies; he also had a mind better fitted than either Schapper or Bauer for the understanding of theoretical issues. I made their

APPENDICES

acquaintance in London during 1843. They were the first proletarian revolutionists I had ever met, and although our outlooks differed in certain details in those early days (for what they had in the way of narrow-minded equalitarian communism[1] was amply compensated in me by a no less narrow-minded philosophical arrogance!), I can never forget the profound impression these three men made upon me, a youngster at the time, just entering upon manhood.

In London, as to a lesser degree in Switzerland, freedom of association and of public meeting was of inestimable advantage to them in their activities. On February 7th, 1840, the German Workers' Educational Society was founded. This was not an underground organisation but functioned in the full light of day. At the time of writing [1885] it is still in existence. The society served as a recruiting-ground for the Federation; and, since the communists were the most active and the most intelligent members of the Society, as always they took it as a matter of course that the leadership of the Society should be in the hands of the Federation. Very soon the Federation could boast of several " communes," or as they were then called " huts," in London. Here, as in Switzerland and elsewhere, tactics were dictated by circumstances. Wherever workers' associations could be formed they were made use of in much the same way. Where legal prohibitions prevented such methods, the organisations took the form of choral societies, gymnastic societies, and the like. Communications were kept up mainly by a continuous flow of travelling members going to and fro among the groups. Where necessary, these travelling members functioned as emissaries. In either case the activity of the Federation was greatly furthered by the governments of the day, which in their wisdom, by exiling every workman who had earned their disfavour—and in nine cases out of ten such a worker was a member of the Federation—converted him into an emissary.

The reconstituted Federation grew apace. In Switzerland this growth was particularly noticeable. Here such men as Weitling (1808-70), August Becker (1814-75), an extremely gifted man, but one whose temperamental instability brought him to grief, just as similar infirmity of purpose had doomed so many

---

[1] By " equalitarian communism " I mean a theory of communism which is exclusively or mainly founded upon a demand for equality.

other Germans), and others formed a strong organisation whose principles were more or less adapted from Weitling's communistic system. This is not the place to discuss Weitling's communism. But, in order to show the importance of Weitling's system as the first stirring of an independent philosophy of the German proletariat, I cannot do better than quote Marx's own words. Here is what he wrote in the Paris *Vorwärts* of 1844: " Where could the German bourgeoisie, including its philosophers and divines, point to a work championing bourgeois political emancipation which could in any way compare with Weitling's *Garantien der Harmonie und Freiheit* [Guarantees of Harmony and Freedom] ? One who compares the jejune and faint-hearted mediocrity of German political literature with this tremendous and brilliant début of the German working class, one who compares the huge baby-shoes of the proletariat with the dwarfed and down-at-heel political shoes of the bourgeoisie, cannot but prophesy that Cinderella will grow to giant stature." The colossus stands before us to-day, and he has many years yet to grow before he will have attained his full proportions.

Many groups were formed in Germany which from their very nature could not be expected to persist. But those that perished were replaced by fresh groups which outnumbered the losses among the more transient ones. Not until 1846, seven years after the first groups had come into existence, did the German police discover in Berlin (Mentel, born 1812) and in Magdeburg (Beck) vestiges of the Federation. But the authorities were not in a position to follow up their discoveries.

Before leaving Paris and fleeing to Switzerland, Weitling had, in 1840, gathered the scattered elements of the Federation together.

The nucleus of the Federation was composed of tailors. Germans practising tailoring business were to be found everywhere: in Switzerland, London, Paris. In the latter town, German was so much the speech of the trade that in 1846 I knew a Norwegian tailor who had journeyed by sea from Drontheim to France, and who had, during eighteen months, hardly spoken a word of French, although he had learned to speak German excellently. In 1847, there were two " communes " of the Federation in Paris. One was mainly composed of tailors, the other of furniture makers.

No sooner was the centre of gravity transferred from Paris to

APPENDICES

London than a new phenomenon came to the fore. The Federation, from being a German organisation, gradually became transformed into an international affair. In addition to German and Swiss, persons of other nationalities to whom the German language could serve as a medium of communication were to be found in the Federation: there were Scandinavians, Dutch, Hungarians, Bohemians, southern Slavs; also there were Russians and Alsatians. In 1847, a British grenadier in full uniform was a regular attendant at the meetings. Soon the Federation was rechristened Communist Workers' Educational Society. On the membership cards we find the following slogan: " All men are brothers " in at least twenty languages, although some of the translations might have been bettered! Besides this society which functioned in the open, there was also a secret organisation. This, too, soon assumed an international character. At first the international aspect was limited in scope; it was forced upon the Federation by the mixed nationalities of its members, and by the gradual realisation that, for the revolution to be effective, it needs must take place on a European scale. Thus far, but no further. Nevertheless the foundations of internationalism were laid.

Those who had fought in the insurrectionary movement of May 1839, and had sought refuge in London, formed a link between the members of the Federation and the French revolutionists. Similarly in the case of the Polish radicals. The more conspicuous Polish refugees, however, people in the public eye, were of course—like Mazzini (1805-72) among the Italian refugees—hostile rather than friendly to the communists. The Chartists, because of the specifically British nature of their movement, were ignored by the Federation as unrevolutionary. At a later date I was able to bring them into touch with the leaders of the Federation in London.

Circumstances led to yet other alterations in the character of the Federation. As was meet in those days, Paris was still looked upon as the birthplace of the revolution. But the movement had now cut loose from the Parisian conspirators. As the Federation grew in size so, likewise, did it grow in the consciousness of its own functions. More and more did its members come to feel that the principles advocated by the Federation were taking root among the German working class, and that the German workers were destined to be the standard-bearers of the European workers as a whole, whether they hailed from the north or from the east. Weitling was a theoretician of communism, who could rank with his French rivals as an equal. The experience of May 12th, 1839, had at last taught the lesson that the policy of abortive risings was useless. Although every event was still looked upon as the possible starting-point of a revolutionary outbreak, although the old, semi-conspirational rules were kept in their integrity, this was no more than a remnant of revolutionary defiance which was already coming into collision with wiser and better outlooks.

The social theories of the Federation, in so far as they existed at all, were wrong-headed. This was due to the conditions of the time. The proletarian part of the membership consisted entirely of manual workers. They were exploited by men who, even in the great metropolis, were nearly always small masters. The exploitation of large-scale tailoring, so-called " confection," the transformation of the work into domestic industry on behalf of a great capitalist, was still in its infancy in the London of that epoch. The exploiter was a small master, and the workers in the trade lived in hopes of themselves becoming small masters. In addition, vestiges of the guild spirit still adhered to the German craftsmen. They were not as yet fully fledged proletarians, were only on the way of becoming members of the modern proletariat, were still hangers-on of the petty bourgeoisie, the large-scale capitalists. These craftsmen, to their eternal honour, instinctively foresaw the future development of their class, and, though not fully conscious of the fact, were pressing forward toward organising themselves as the party of the proletariat. Yet it was impossible to expect that their ingrained craft prejudices should not occasionally trip them up, especially when it came to a detailed criticism of extant society, that is to say, when the investigation of economic facts was demanded of them. I do not believe that one single member of the Federation had ever read a book on political economy. No matter! " Equality," " Brotherhood," " Justice," gave them a leg over every theoretical stile!

Alongside the communist theory devised by the Federation and by Weitling, another, and very different, theory of communism was emerging. While living in Manchester, I was made painfully aware that economic factors, hitherto assigned an insignificant role or no role at all by historians, were, at least under modern conditions, a decisive power in the world; that they were the cause of contemporary class antagonisms; that in lands where, on account of great industrial developments (as in England), these antagonisms have come into the open, they are creating a new political party, fresh party struggles, and, consequently, are completely changing the face of political life. Already in 1844, writing in the *Deutsch-Französische Jahrbücher*, Marx showed that he had come to the same conclusions. He maintained that it was not the State which conditioned and regulated bourgeois society, but, rather, bourgeois society which conditioned and regulated the State; that, therefore, politics and the history of political development must be examined in the light of economic conditions and their evolution, not the other way about as heretofore. When I visited Marx in Paris during the summer of 1844, it was obvious that we were in complete harmony as far as theoretical matters were concerned. From that time our working partnership may be dated. When in the spring of 1845 we met again, this time in Brussels, Marx had already elaborated the main points in his materialist theory of history. Now we set about the task of working the theory out in its manifold details.

This theory, which was to revolutionise the science of history, this theory for which Marx is mainly responsible (for I played a very insignificant part in the matter), was of the utmost importance to the contemporary working-class movement. Communism, among the French and the Germans, Chartism, among the Britishers, were now no longer to be looked upon as chance phenomena which might just as well not have appeared at all. These movements were seen to be an expression of the aspirations of an oppressed class, one that had arisen as the outcome of modern life, the class of the proletariat; they appeared as more or less developed forms of a historically necessary struggle against the ruling class, the bourgeoisie. Nevertheless, as forms of the class struggle, they differed from earlier class struggles in the following particular: the oppressed class to-day, the proletariat, cannot achieve its own emancipation without liberating the whole of society from class divisions. The victory of the proletariat will bring the class war to an end. Communism no longer signified the fantastical elaboration of a social ideal as nearly achieving perfection as possible. On the contrary. Communism meant henceforward an understanding of the nature, the conditions, and the general aims arising therefrom, of the struggle into which the proletariat had entered.

We had no wish to propound these new scientific conclusions in ponderous tomes for the edification of professional wiseacres. Quite otherwise. We had both of us entered bag and baggage into the political movement, we had certain connections with the educated world (especially in the western provinces of Germany), and had close ties with the organised proletariat. In duty bound, we had to place our outlook upon a firm scientific foundation; but it was no less incumbent upon us to win over the European proletariat in general and the German proletariat in particular to our convictions. No sooner had we made the matter clear to ourselves than we set to work. We founded the German Workers' Society of Brussels, and took possession of the *Deutsche Brüsseler Zeitung*. This periodical remained in our hands until the February revolution. Through the intermediation of Julian Harney we got into touch with the Chartists. I contributed to the *Northern Star*, the central organ of the Chartist movement, whose editor was Harney. We also collaborated with the Brussels democrats. Indeed, Marx was vice-president of the German section of the Democratic League, an international organisation founded in Brussels. Further, we linked up with the French democrats who were running a newspaper called *La Réforme*, to which I was a contributor. In a word, our relations with radical and proletarian organisations and journals left nothing to be desired.

Our relations with the Federation of the Just were as follows. Of course we knew of the existence of this body. Schapper had suggested that I become a member as long ago as 1843. But for obvious reasons, I had refused his invitation. Nevertheless, we kept up a lively correspondence with the London " commune," and were even more closely associated with Dr. Everbeck, who was then the leading figure in the Paris " communes." Without troubling ourselves about the internal situation of the Federation we were nevertheless kept informed as to every important issue. By word of mouth, by letters, through the newspapers, we pressed our theoretical outlook upon the notice of the members. In addition we issued lithographed circulars on special occasions (as, for instance, in connection with the internal affairs of the communist party now in process of formation), and posted these to our friends and correspondents the world over.

I

APPENDICES

A young student, Hermann Kriege (1820-1850) by name, from Westphalia, emigrated to America. He gave himself out to be an emissary from the Federation, associated with the madcap Harro Harring, and, with the prestige of the Federation to back him, proposed to inagurate the revolution in South America. He founded a newspaper in which he expounded, in the name of the Federation, an extravagantly sentimental form of communism based upon love, overflowing with love. We immediately sallied forth to the attack by means of a circular which did not fail of its effect. As far as the Federation was concerned, Kriege was heard of no more.

Later, Weitling came to Brussels. But he was no longer the simple-hearted young journeyman tailor, who, rather awed by his own talents, had once been so eager to get a clear picture of just what a communist world would look like. He was now the great man whose superiority made him the butt of the envious, one who was ever suspecting his rivals, his secret enemies, of laying traps to snare him; a prophet hounded from one country to another; a seer who had recipe ready to hand for the realisation of heaven upon earth, and fancied that every one he encountered was trying to steal it from him. He had already become embroiled with the members of the Federation in London and in Brussels. In the latter town Marx and his wife had welcomed Weitling with well-nigh superhuman forbearance. But Weitling could not get on with any one. He left for the States, hoping that there he would be able to continue his prophetic mission.

All these manifold circumstances contributed their quota to bringing about a change in the Federation. The changed outlooks were particularly noticeable among the London members. From the theoretical side, the inadequacy both of French equalitarian communism and of Weitling's brand of communism was becoming plainer day by day. Weitling's endeavour to bring back communism to early Christian practice—such luminous suggestions are, in very truth, to be found in his " gospel of poor sinners "—had, in Switzerland, either thrown the movement into the hands of a fool like Albrecht (1809-1872) or condemned it to exploitation by bogus prophets like Kuhlmann. " True socialism " [see the section of the Manifesto dealing with " German or True Socialism "], the affectation of a few men of letters,

APPENDICES

was no more than the translation of French socialist expressions into Hegelian German sicklied over with sentimental effusions about love. It had been introduced into the Federation by Kriege and other readers of the relevant literature, and by now the slobbering spinelessness of the doctrine was disgusting the veteran revolutionists of the Federation. The theoretical ideas hitherto held were obviously becoming untenable, and the errors arising out of these theories were more and more clearly defined. Consequently, those responsible for the Federation in London were increasingly convinced that the new theories put forward by Marx and myself were correct. Undoubtedly the growth of this conviction was fostered by two men who happened to be members of the London " commune " at the time, two men who far outstripped the other leaders in theoretical competence. These were Karl Pfänder (died 1876), the miniature painter from Heilbronn, and Georg Eccarius (died 1889), the tailor from Thüringen. [1]

To cut a long story short, Moll came to Brussels in the spring of 1847. He visited Marx, and then came on to Paris to see me. His mission was to invite us once more, at the urgent request of his comrades, to enter the federation. They were all convinced of the general correctness of our views, and no less convinced were they that the time had come for ridding the Federation of its traditional forms and conspirational methods. Should we enter the Federation, we should be given an opportunity, at a congress, to lay our theories of communism before the members in the shape of a manifesto, which would then be published as the manifesto of the Federation. Thus, he continued, we should be contributing to the replacement of the old Federation by an organisation more in keeping with the time and with our common aims.

We were in no doubt as to the need of an organisation for the purpose of carrying on propaganda among the German workers; nor did we fail to realise that such an organisation in so far as it was not of a purely local character, would have to be a secret one even outside the German frontiers. Now, just such an organisation already existed in the shape of the Federation. What we had

---

[1] Pfänder died in London about eight years ago [1876]. He was a man of fine intelligence, original, full of fun, ironical, dialectical. Eccarius acted for many years as general secretary of the International Workingmen's Association, on whose General Council we find such names as Eccarius, Pfänder, Lessner (1825-1910), Lochner (b. 1826), Marx, my own. Subsequently Eccarius devoted himself entirely to the trade union movement in Britain.

APPENDICES

hitherto been condemning was now recognised by the Federation itself as erroneous; we ourselves were asked to help in the work of reorganisation. Could we refuse? Certainly not. We became members of the Federation. From among our own friends in Brussels, Marx was able to found a " commune." For my part, I visited the three " communes " which existed in Paris.

In the summer of 1847 the first congress of the Federation took place in London. Wilhelm Wolff was the delegate from the Brussels " commune," and I represented the Paris " communes." The main theme for discussion was the question of reorganisation. Every vestige of its old mystical nature, the heritage of conspirational days, was now discarded. The Federation was organised into communes, circles, leading circles, central committee, and congress. It took the name of Communist League. The first article of the convention runs: " The aim of the League is the overthrow of the bourgeoisie, the establishment of the rule of the proletariat, the abolition of the bourgeois social order founded upon class antagonisms, and the inauguration of a new social order wherein there shall be neither classes nor private property." The organisation was democratic through and through; its officials were elected and were subject to recall. This alone was sufficient to put an end to any hankering to revert to conspiratorial methods, for these require a dictatorship if they are to be successful. Thus, at least in so far as times of peace were concerned, the Federation was transformed into a propaganda society. The new rules—so democratic had we all become—were laid before the " communes " for discussion. They were further considered at the second congress, and were finally accepted by this body on December 8th, 1847. They may be found, printed in full, in Wermuth and Stieber's (1818-1882) work on the communist conspiracies of the nineteenth century, vol. i, p. 239, appendix viii.

The second congress took place during the last days of November and the early days of December of the same year. This time, Marx was present and explained the new theory in the course of a lengthy debate—the congress sat for ten days at the lowest reckoning. Contradiction and doubt were set at rest, the new theory was unanimously accepted, and Marx and I were commissioned to draw up a manifesto. We completed our task without delay. A few weeks before the outbreak of the February revolution, the manuscript was sent to London where it was printed. Since that time it has made the voyage round the world, has been translated into almost every language, and even to this day serves as a guide to the proletarian movement in the most diverse countries. The motto of the Federation: " All men are brothers," was replaced by a new slogan: " Proletarians of all lands, unite." This was a public declaration of the international character of the struggle. Seventeen years later this war-cry resounded throughout the world as the watchword of the International Workingmen's Association, and to-day the struggling proletariat in all lands has inscribed it on its banner.

APPENDIX II

DEMANDS OF THE COMMUNIST PARTY IN GERMANY

Motto: Proletarians of all lands, unite!

1. The whole of Germany shall be declared to be a one and indivisible republic.

2. Every German, having attained the age of 21, and provided he has not been a condemned criminal, shall be eligible both for election and as elector.

3. Representatives of the people shall be salaried so that manual workers, too, shall be able to become members of the German parliament.

4. Universal arming of the people. In future the army shall be simultaneously a worker-army, so that the military arm shall not, as in the past, merely consume, but shall produce more than is actually necessary for its upkeep.

This will likewise be an aid to the organisation of labour.

5. Gratuitous legal services.

6. All feudal dues, exactions, corvées, tithes, etc., which have hitherto pressed upon the rural population, shall be abolished without compensation.

7. Royal and other feudal domains, together with mines, pits, and so forth, shall become the property of the State. The domains shall be cultivated on the large scale and with the most up-to-date scientific devices in the interests of the whole of society.

8. Mortgages on peasant lands shall be declared the property of the State. Interest on such mortgages shall be paid by the peasant to the State as a tax.

9. In localities where farming methods are well developed, the landrent or the earnest money shall be paid to the State as a tax.

The measures advocated in Nos. 6, 7, 8 and 9 have been put forward with a view to decreasing the burdens hitherto imposed upon the peasantry and the small farmers, without cutting down the means available for defraying State expenses and without imperilling production.

The landed proprietor who is neither a peasant nor a farmer, has no share in production. Consumption on his part is, therefore, unwarrantable.

10. A State bank, whose paper issues are legal tender, shall replace the many private banking concerns now in existence.

By this method credit can be regulated in the interest of the people as a whole, and thereby the dominion of the magnates of the monetary world will be undermined. Further, by gradually substituting paper money for gold and silver coin, the means of exchange (that indispensable prerequisite of bourgeois trade and commerce) will be cheapened, and gold and silver will be set free for use in foreign commerce. This measure in the long run is necessary in order to blind the interests of the conservative bourgeoisie to the cause of the revolution.

11. All the means of transport, railways, waterways, steamships, roads, etc., shall be taken over by the State. They shall become the property of the State and shall be placed at the disposal of the non-possessing classes gratuitously, for their own use.

12. Salaries of all civil servants shall be identical, except in the case where a civil servant has a family to support. His requirements being greater, his salary shall be higher.

13. Complete separation of Church and State. The clergy of every denomination shall be paid by the voluntary contributions of their congregations.

14. The right of inheritance to be curtailed.

15. The introduction of a steeply graduated income tax, and the abolition of taxes on articles of consumption.

16. Inauguration of national workshops. The State guarantees a livelihood to all workers and provides for those who are incapacitated for work.

17. Universal and gratuitous education.

It is to the interest of the German proletariat, the petty bourgeoisie, and the small peasantry to support these demands with all possible energy. Only by the realisation of these demands will the millions in Germany who have hitherto been exploited by a handful of persons and whom the exploiters would fain still keep

APPENDICES

in subjection, win the rights and attain to the power which they, as the producers of all wealth, are entitled to expect.

The Committee:

KARL MARX KARL SCHAPPER
H. BAUER   F. ENGELS
J. MOLL   W. WOLFF

APPENDIX III

FIRST ADDRESS OF THE CENTRAL COMMITTEE OF THE COMMUNIST LEAGUE TO ITS MEMBERS IN GERMANY

BROTHERS—in the two revolutionary years of 1848-9, the Communist League has stood the test in dual fashion—once through the fact that its members everywhere had taken hold of the movement energetically, and had stood foremost in the ranks of the only decisive revolutionary class, the proletariat, in the publication of the Press, on the barricades and on the battlefields. The League had further proved its worth, because its comprehension of the movement, as it was laid down in the circular letter sent out by the Congress and the Central Committee containing the Communist Manifesto of 1847, had proved to be the only correct one in that the expectations expressed in that official document had been completely fulfilled and that its conception of present-day social relations (which previously had been only secretly advocated by the League) is now on the lips of the nations and is openly preached on the public squares. At the same time the previously strong organisation of the League has been seriously shattered. A large part of the membership, which had directly participated in the revolutionary movement, believed that the necessity for secret societies was over and that public activities alone were sufficient. The individual circles and (fellowship) societies permitted their connections with the Central Committee to slacken, and gradually broke off altogether.

While the Democratic Party, the party of the petty bourgeoisie, organised itself more and more in Germany, the workers' party lost its only strong footing and remained organised at the most in a few localities for local purposes only, and was, therefore, completely subordinated in the general movement to the rule and guidance of the petty-bourgeois Democrats. An end must now be made to these conditions and the independent activity of the workers must be re-established. The Central Committee realised this necessity, and, therefore, sent an emissary, Joseph Moll, to Germany in the winter of 1848-9 for the purpose of reorganising the League. This mission of Moll's did not accomplish any lasting results, partly because the German workers at that time had not had enough experience and partly because the insurrection of last May interrupted the carrying out of this mission. Moll himself took up arms, entered the army of Baden-Pfalz and fell on July 19th in the battle of the Murg. The League sustained a loss of one of its oldest, most active and trustworthy members, who had participated in all party congresses and Central Committee meetings and had previously carried out a series of secret missions with great success. After the defeat of the revolutionary parties of Germany and France in 1849, practically all the members of the Central Committee, supplied with new revolutionary energy, reassembled again in London and urged on the reorganisation of the League with renewed zeal.

This reorganisation can only succeed through an emissary and the Central Committee especially considers it of the highest importance that the emissary should leave at this moment when a new revolution is approaching, when the workers' party must be as well organised as possible and must appear in the arena as united and as independent as possible if it is not to be exploited and taken in tow by the bourgeoisie as was the case in 1848.

Brothers! We told you as early as 1848 that the German Liberal bourgeoisie would soon come into power and would immediately turn its newly-achieved power against the workers. You have seen how this prophecy was fulfilled. In reality it was the bourgeoisie who, after the March movement of 1848, took possession of the State power and used this power to throw back the workers, its recent allies, into their former oppressed position. If the bourgeoisie could not do this without entering into an alliance with the feudal party, which had been put aside in March, without even finally yielding again to the rule of this feudal absolutist party, then it had still got for itself conditions which, in view of the government's financial embarrassments, would have given it power for a long time and have guaranteed all its interests in case it had appeared possible that the revolutionary movement was already entering on the path of so-called peaceful development. To guarantee its rule the bourgeoisie would not even have needed to apply violent measures and thus rouse the hatred of the people, since all these measures had been taken already by the feudal counter-revolution. But development is not going along this peaceful course. On the contrary, the revolution is near which will accelerate that development, whether it is caused by an independent rising of the French proletariat or the invasion of the Holy Alliance against the revolutionary Babylon.[1]

And the role, this traitorous role, which the German Liberal bourgeoisie of 1848 played against the people will be taken over by the democratic petty bourgeoisie who, as an opposition party, will take the same position in the approaching revolution, as did the Liberal bourgeoisie of 1848.

This Democratic Party, which is far more dangerous to the workers than the Liberals were previously, is composed of three elements:

1. Of the most progressive parts of the great bourgeoisie, who have as their aim the immediate and complete overthrow of feudalism and absolutism. This faction is represented by the late Berliner Vereinbaren—the tax-objectors.

2. Of the constitutional democratic petty bourgeoisie whose principal purpose during the recent movement was the establishment of a more or less democratic United States of Germany as striven for by its representatives in the left fraction of the Frankfort Assembly, later in the Stuttgart Assembly, and in the campaign for the Federal Constitution.

3. Of the republican petty bourgeoisie, whose ideal is a German federated republic, after the manner of Switzerland, and who now call themselves " Red " and " Social-Democratic," because they cherish the pious wish to abolish the pressure of the large bourgeoisie against the petty bourgeoisie. The representatives of this faction were the members of the Democratic Congress and Committee, the directors of the Democratic societies and the editors of the Democratic newspapers.

All these factions since their defeat call themselves " Republicans " or " Reds," just as the republican petty bourgeoisie in Frankfort now call themselves " Socialists." But where, as in Würtemberg, Bavaria, etc., they still find the opportunity to accomplish their purposes by constitutional means, they take advantage of this opportunity to stow away their old phrases, and

---

[1] i. e. France.—ED.

APPENDICES

prove that in practice they have not changed in the slightest. It further stands to reason that the altered name of this party does not change their relationship to the workers in the slightest degree, but it simply proves that when they have to act against the bourgeoisie which is in alliance with absolutism they are compelled to lean on the proletariat for aid.

The petty bourgeois Democratic Party in Germany is very powerful; it includes not only the great majority of the middle-class population of the cities—the small industrial merchants and the guild masters, it also includes the peasantry and the land proletariat in its following, so long as the latter has not yet found a support in the independent proletariat of the cities.

The circumstances in which the revolutionary workers' party finds itself, make it go hand-in-hand with the petty bourgeois Democratic Party against the faction which it proposes to overthrow, but the party of the workers assumes the attitude of opposition in all matters where the petty bourgeoisie wishes to secure its own position.

The democratic petty bourgeoisie, which is far from desiring to revolutionise the whole of society for the proletariat, strives for a change in social conditions whereby the present society will be made as bearable and as comfortable as possible for itself. It, therefore, desires above all to decrease the governmental expenditure through restriction on the bureaucracy and the imposition of the principal taxes on the large landowners and bourgeoisie. It further demands the removal of the pressure of large capital upon small capital through the establishment of public credit institutions and the passage of laws against usurers through which it will be possible to obtain loans for itself and for the peasantry on more favourable terms than from the capitalists. It further desires the establishment of bourgeois property relationship on the land through the complete abolition of feudalism. In order to carry all this through it requires a democratic, that is, a constitutional republican government which would give it and its allies, the peasantry, the majority, and a democratic municipal system of Government which would place in their hands direct control over municipal property and over a series of political functions (political offices) which are now exercised by the bureaucrats.

The rule of capital and its quick growth would be further

counteracted by them partly through the restriction of the right of inheritance and partly by the assumption of as many public works by the State as possible. As far as the workers are concerned, it remains definite that they are to remain in the same position as heretofore, only the democratic petty bourgeoisie desires to secure for the workers a better wage and a more secure existence; it hopes to achieve this purpose through temporary employment of workers by the State and through welfare measures. In short it hopes to bribe the workers more or less through indirect alms, and to break their revolutionary energy by momentarily rendering their condition bearable. The demands of the petty bourgeois democracy, herein included, are not made simultaneously by all its factions, but taken as a whole they are the established goal of a few of its adherents. The further individuals or fractions go in their demands the greater the number of these which become their own demands; the few who see in the above demands their own programme may think that this is the maximum which can be demanded from the revolution. These demands can in no way satisfy the party of the proletariat.

While the democratic petty bourgeoisie wishes to bring the revolution to as swift a conclusion as possible through the carrying out at the most of the above-mentioned demands, it is in our interest and it is our task to make the revolution permanent until all propertied classes are more or less dispossessed, the governmental power acquired by the proletariat and the association of proletarians, achieved not only in one country, but in all important countries of the world, thus ending the competition of the proletariat in these countries and at least until the most important productive forces are concentrated in the hands of the proletariat. With us it cannot be a mere matter of a change in the form of private property, but of destroying it as an institution; not in hushing up class antagonisms but in abolishing all classes; not in the improvement of present-day society but in the foundation of a new society. There is no doubt whatsoever that petty bourgeois democracy will for the moment acquire a preponderating influence during the development of the revolution in Germany. The question therefore arises, what should be the attitude of the proletariat and especially the League of Communists towards the petty bourgeois democracy:

APPENDICES

1. During the continuation of the present relations when the petty bourgeois Democrats are still oppressed?

2. In the coming revolutionary struggle, during which the petty bourgeois Democrats will obtain the preponderance of power?

3. After the struggle during the period when the petty bourgeois democrats will exercise their preponderance of power over the classes that have just been overthrown and over the proletariat?

First: At the moment when the democratic petty bourgeoisie are everywhere oppressed, they in general preach unity and reconciliation with the proletariat; they try to tie its hands and strive to create a great opposition party that will include all shades of opinion in the democratic party—which means that they strive to entangle the workers in a party organisation in which general Social-Democratic phrases predominate and behind which their special class interests are hidden. But the definite demands of the proletariat must, of course, for the sake of peace and tranquillity, not be brought forward. Such a unity would only accrue to their advantage entirely and to the disadvantage of the proletariat. The proletariat would lose its whole independent position bought at such a steep price and would sink down to be again an appendage of the official bourgeois democracy.

This unity must be rejected in a most decisive manner. Instead of letting themselves out to the bourgeois Democrats to serve them as a sort of applauding choir, the workers (and above all the League) must work for the establishment of an independent secret and open organisation of the worker's party side by side with the official Democrats, and make every municipality a centre and a nucleus of workers' societies, in which the position and interests of the proletariat should be discussed independently of bourgeois influences.

How earnest the bourgeois Democrats are in the desire for an alliance can be seen from the example of the Breslau Democrats who in their organ *Neue Oder Zeitung* attack the independently organised workers, whom they call " Socialists," in the most rabid manner.

In the case where a struggle against a common enemy exists a special kind of alliance is unnecessary. As soon as it becomes necessary to fight such an enemy directly, the interests of both

APPENDICES

parties fall together for the moment; and this momentary connection will be established in the future as it has been in the past. It is understood that in the coming bloody conflicts, as in all the previous ones, it will be the workers principally who will achieve victory by their courage, decisiveness and self-sacrifice. As before, the petty bourgeoisie, *en masse*, will again hesitate to enter this struggle; keeping themselves inactive and undecided as long as possible. And then, as soon as victory has been decided, they will endeavour to annex it for themselves. They will call upon the workers to keep the peace and return to their work in order to avoid (so-called) excesses; and then proceed to cut the workers off from the fruits of victory. It does not lie in the power of the workers to prevent the petty bourgeoisie from doing this; but it does lie in their power to make it as difficult as possible for the petty bourgeoisie to use their power against the armed proletariat, and to dictate such conditions to them, that the rule of the bourgeois Democrats will beforehand carry within itself the germ of its own destruction, so that their displacement later by the rule of the proletariat will be made considerably easier.

During the conflict and immediately after the struggle, the workers must counteract, above all things and in so far as it is at all possible, bourgeois appeals for peace by forcing the Democrats to carry out themselves their present terroristic phrases. They must strive so that the revolutionary excitement immediately manifesting itself is not suppressed again immediately after the victory. On the contrary they must maintain it as long as possible. Far from coming out against the so-called excesses (instances of popular revenge against hated individuals or public buildings which are bound up with hated reminiscences) it is not merely necessary to tolerate these examples, but it will be necessary to take them into their own hands and direct them.

During the struggle and after the struggle, the workers at every opportunity must put up their own demands in contradistinction to the demands put forward by the bourgeois Democrats. They must demand guarantees for the workers as soon as the bourgeois Democrats get ready to take over the government into their own hands. In case of necessity, they must obtain these guarantees by force, and especially they must see to it that the new rulers should bind themselves to as many concessions and pledges as possible. The surest way is to force them to compromise themselves. They

APPENDICES

must check as far as possible all manifestations of intoxication for the victory and enthusiasm for the new state of affairs which set in after every victorious street battle, and must express candidly their lack of confidence in the new government in every way through a cold-blooded analysis of the new state of affairs. They must simultaneously erect their own revolutionary workers' government hard by the new official government whether it be in the form of executive committees, community councils, workers' clubs or workers' committees, so that the bourgeoisie democratic government not only will lose its immediate restraint over the workers, but, on the contrary, must at once feel themselves watched over and threatened by an authority behind which stand the mass of the workers. In a word: from the first moment of the victory, and after it, the distrust of the workers must not be directed any more against the conquered reactionary party, but against their previous ally, the petty bourgeois Democrats, who desire to exploit the common victory only for themselves.

Second: But in order to be able to oppose this party (whose treason to the workers will start from the very first hour of the victory) with energy and menaces the workers must be armed and organised. The arming of the whole proletariat with muskets, rifles, cannon and munitions must be carried through immediately, and the revival of the old Citizens' Guard, directed against the workers, must be opposed. Where it is not possible, however, to carry through this latter objective, the workers must attempt to organise themselves independently as proletarian guards with their own chiefs and a general staff elected by themselves and to place themselves not under the orders of the existing State power, but under the revolutionary community-councils, organised through the efforts of the workers. Where workers are employed by the State they must organise and arm themselves into a special corps with a self-elected chief or as a part of the proletarian guard. The workers must not permit their arms and munitions to be taken out of their hands under any pretext; every attempt to disarm the proletariat must be frustrated by force if necessary. The destruction of the influence of the bourgeois Democrats upon the workers: immediate, independent and armed organisation of the workers; the creation of conditions that will be as burdensome and as compromising as possible for the bourgeois democracy, whose momentary rule will be inevitable; these are the principal points which the proletariat and also the League must keep in mind during the approaching uprising.

Third: As soon as the new government has established itself, the struggle against the workers will begin. In order that the workers should be able to oppose the democratic petty bourgeoisie with force, it is necessary above all that they should be independently organised in clubs and centralised. The Central Committee of the League will come to Germany as quickly as possible, soon after the overthrow of the present government, and will immediately convene a congress and lay before it the necessary proposals for the centralisation of the workers' clubs, under a directorship functioning from the central point of the movement. The quick organisation of provincial connections of the workers' clubs is one of the most important points in the strengthening and development of the workers' party. The immediate consequences of the overthrow of the existing government will be the election of a national representative body. The proletariat must here take care of the following:

1. Not to permit any large number of workers to be excluded from voting under any kind of pretext through the chicanery of the local authorities and government commissioners.

2. The workers' candidates, who should consist as far as possible of members of the League, should be put up in opposition to those of the petty bourgeois Democratic candidates. The election of our candidates is to be striven for by all possible means. Even in those localities where there is no prospect of carrying them through the workers must put up their own candidates in order to preserve their own independence, in order to be able to calculate their own forces and in order to bring their revolutionary attitude and party standpoint before the public mind. They must not permit themselves to be corrupted by the phrases of the Democrats, as for example, that the Democratic party will be split because of the independent action of the workers, and that it will make possible the victory of the reaction. When such phrases are used, the final result is that the proletariat will always be swindled. The progress which the proletarian party must make through such independent appearance is infinitely more important than the disadvantage accruing from the presence of several reactionaries in the representative body. If the proletarian democ-

K

racy comes out in the very beginning with determination and with terroristic acts against the reaction the influence of the reaction at the elections will moreover be destroyed in advance.

The first point at which the bourgeois Democrats will come into conflict with the workers will be on the question of the abolition of feudalism. As in the first French Revolution the petty bourgeois will give the feudal lands freely to the peasantry, that means that it will permit the agrarian proletariat to remain in the same position as heretofore, as they desire a petty bourgeois peasant class which will go through the same cycle of impoverishment and indebtedness with which the French peasantry is now afflicted.

In the interest of the proletariat the workers must come out in opposition to this plan. They must demand that the confiscated feudal property should be converted into State farms to be used as labour colonies, which the agrarian proletariat should exploit with all the advantages of large-scale farming, and through which the principle of collective property should immediately achieve a strong basis in the midst of the weakening bourgeois property relationships. The workers must combine with the land proletariat just as the Democrats combine with the peasantry. The Democrats will further work either for the establishment of a federated republic or in case they are not in a position to avoid the establishment of the republic one and indivisible, will seek to paralyse the central government by demanding the utmost autonomy and independence for the municipalities and provinces. In opposition to this plan the workers must strive not only for the establishment of the German republic, one and indivisible, but also for the most decisive centralisation of force in the hands of the State. They must not permit themselves to be fooled by the Democrats' talk of freedom for the local communities, self-government, etc. In a country like Germany where there are so many of the remains of feudalism to be abolished, where so many local and provincial individualisms must be broken up, it must under no circumstances be tolerated that every village, city and province should become a hindrance to revolutionary activity, which can only be developed to its full power from one central point. It must not be tolerated that the present conditions should be re-enacted whereby the Germans must fight separately in every city and province for the same amount of progress.

Still less is it possible to permit the perpetuation of municipal property which is a more reactionary form than contemporary private property, which now is everywhere in decay and becoming private property and the cause of constant litigation between rich and poor municipalities; it is also impermissible that alongside with the general state civil law the existing municipal civil law with its cavilling at the workers should be perpetuated through the so-called free construction of the commune. At the present day it is the task of a really revolutionary party to carry through the strictest centralisation as was the case in France in 1793.[1]

We have seen how the Democrats may be expected to come into power at the next revolutionary movement, how they will be compelled to propose more or less Socialistic measures. It will be asked what measures should the workers propose in contrast. In the beginning of the movement, the workers will naturally not be able to propose any direct Communist measures, however they can:

1. Compel the Democrats to encroach as far as possible upon the existing system of society in order to interfere with its regular development and thus make them compromise their own position, thus to force as many of the productive forces, transportation, means, factories, railroads, as possible to be concentrated into the hands of the State.

2. They must drive the proposals of the Democrats, which in

[1] It must be observed to-day that this remark is based on a misunderstanding. It was then considered an established fact—thanks to Bonapartist and liberal falsifiers of history, that the French centralised apparatus of administration was introduced by the Great Revolution and that the Convention used it as an essential and decisive weapon in the fight with the Royalist and federalist reaction and with external enemies. But it is now a well-known fact that throughout the revolution right up to the 18th Brumaire the whole administration of the departments, districts and municipalities consisted of authorities elected by the population itself which had full freedom within the limits of general state legislation. This provincial and local self-government, like the American, was the revolution's strongest lever and so much so that Napoleon, immediately after his *coup d'état* of the 18th Brumaire, hastened to replace it by the rule of the prefects which has been kept up to the present day, and which, in this way, was from the beginning a real weapon of the reaction. But in so far as local and provincial self-government does not contradict political and national centralisation, it is to that extent not necessarily bound up with that limited cantonal and municipal egoism which so repels as in Switzerland and which all the South German federal republicans wanted to introduce into Germany in 1849.—(Note by Engels to the Zurich edition of 1885.)

any case are not revolutionary but reformistic, to the extreme and transform these proposals into direct attacks upon private property; as for example, if the petty bourgeoisie propose to buy out the railroads and factories, then the workers must demand that the railroads and factories, since they are the property of the reactionaries, must simply be confiscated by the State without compensation. If the democrats propose proportional taxes they must demand progressive (income) taxes; if the Democrats themselves bring forward a proposal for a moderate progressive (income) tax, then the workers must insist on a tax, the rates of which are so steep that large capital would soon go to smash as a result; if the Democrats demand the regulation of the State debt, the workers must insist upon its repudiation (State bankruptcy). The demands of the workers, therefore, will everywhere depend on the concessions and measures advanced by the Democrats.

Even if the German workers may not be able to attain power and carry through their class interests, then they have the certainty this time that the first act of this approaching revolutionary drama will be simultaneous with the direct victory of their own class in France and will be very much expedited by it.

But they will accomplish the greatest part of their final victory for themselves through self-enlightenment as to their class interests, by taking their own independent party attitude as early as possible, and by not permitting themselves to be fooled as to the necessity for the independent organisation of the party of the proletariat by the hypocritical phrases of the democratic petty bourgeoisie. Their battle-cry must always be, " The Permanent Revolution! "

London, *March* 1850.

GLOSSARY OF NAMES AND PHRASES

ALLIANCE, HOLY: The agreement, ratified September 26th, 1815, between the Emperors of Russia, and Austria, and the King of Prussia, to " be governed by Christian principles in all their political transactions, with a view to perpetuating the peace they had won " (i.e. over the French Revolution). The post-Waterloo anticipation of the League of Nations " only more so." The " holy " object of the Alliance was intervention against all revolutionary movements.

" ANCIEN RÉGIME ": The " old order," things as they were before the French Revolution of 1789.

ANLA, THE: University Building, Vienna.

ARCHDUKE JOHN (OF AUSTRIA): Younger brother of the Emperor Ferdinand II; regarded as of popular sympathies because of his marriage with an inn-keeper's daughter.

AUERSWALD, HANS VON: Prussian General, Member of Frankfurt National Assembly, killed, with Prince Lidnowsky, by villagers near Frankfurt.

BAKUNIN, MICHAEL (1814-76): Born near Moscow of a noble family; resigned commission in Russian army 1838; after leading the fight in Dresden 1848 was handed over to the Tsar, who sent him to Siberia; after escaping thence became the leader of the anarchist opposition to Marx in the First International.

BAN, THE: The " headman " of the Croats (*see* JELLACHICH).

BEM, JOSEPH (1795-1850): Leader in the Polish insurrection of of 1830-1; organised defence of Vienna; served later in the Hungarian insurrection 1848-9; escaped to Turkey, turned Mohammedan and died of a fever.

GLOSSARY

BLANC, LOUIS: French "Democratic-Socialist," became the Minister of Labour in the bourgeois Provisional Government of February 1848; celebrated for his work on the "Organisation of Labour"—his co-operative producing workshops. A typical middle-class Utopian, denounced the workers' insurrection of June 1848, and later denounced also the Commune of 1871.

BLUM, ROBERT (1807-48): Born in poverty in Cologne; became secretary and treasurer to a theatre in Cologne, later a bookseller and publisher in Dresden; one of the most energetic leaders in 1848; sent as head of a delegation from the Frankfurt Assembly to Vienna, he was arrested and shot after court-martial at the express order of Prince Schwartzenburg.

"BOMBA," KING: Ferdinand II of Naples—so-called for his two days' bombardment of Palermo, then in insurrection, February 1848.

BRENTANO, LUDWIG: A Baden lawyer; not to be confounded with the economist Lujo Brentano (b. 1844).

CAMPHAUSEN, LUDOLF: One time president of the Chamber of Commerce, Cologne; Prussian Prime Minister, March 28th, 1848.

CHANGARNIER, NICOLAS ANNE THEODULE (1793-1877): French General, served in the army of occupation in Algiers, 1830 to 1847; in 1848 was appointed Governor-General of Algiers, and later Commandant of the National Guard and the garrisons of Paris. Assisted in organising the butchery of the "Days of June."

CHARLEMAGNE: Charles the Great, King of the Franks and restorer of the Roman Empire; born 742, died 814. His Empire, which originally included most of present-day Austria, Germany, Holland, Belgium, France and part of Spain, was dismembered at his death, but a relic of it survived in the "Holy" Roman Empire which (curtailed considerably and in practice the Empire of Austria) was still in nominal existence until 1804, when the title was formally abandoned.

GLOSSARY

CONFEDERATION (The German): The Union of Germanic States set up June 1815. It included Austria, Prussia, Bavaria, Saxony, Würtemburg, Baden, Hesse, twenty-five smaller States and the Free Towns of Hamburg, Frankfurt, Bremen and Lübeck. It accepted the hegemony of the Austrian Emperor, and was presided over by a Diet, or " College " composed of representatives appointed by the heads of each of the confederated but independent States. It was brought to an end by the defeat of Austria by Prussia, 1866.

CONGREGATIONALISTS, FREE: The then surviving relic of the Anabaptists of the early Reformation period; a sect with affinities to the English Baptists on the one side and Quakers on the other.

CONGRESS OF VIENNA: Met November 1814 to decide the terms of the reconstitution of the European Monarchies (including that of France) after the defeat and exile of Napoleon.

" CONTINENTAL SYSTEM ": Napoleon's plan instituted by the " Berlin decree," 1806, whereby he sought to cut off all commercial traffic between Britain and the Continent.

CRUSADERS, SONS OF THE: Courtesy title given themselves by the Hapsburgs, and the Holenstanper. The Emperors of Austria till the end included " King of Jerusalem " among their many titles.

DAHLMANN, FREDERICK CRISTOPH (1785-1869): German historian; Professor at Kiel 1813, and Göttingen 1829; banished from Hanover 1837; Professor of History at Bonn 1842, headed the Constitutional-Liberals in 1848.

DANTON, GEORGES JACQUES (1759-94): Lawyer, Jacobin leader in the French Revolution; became Minister of Justice on the overthrow of the Monarchy, August 10th, 1792; was one of the original members of the Committee of Public Safety; led the attack in the Convention on the Girondists to the Right, and the Hebertists to the Left; representing the new bourgeoisie, Danton took a stand against the further development of the revolution to the Left, became involved with the counter-revolution, and was guillotined along with his associates.

GLOSSARY

DÉSIRÉ, LOUIS LE (" Louis the Desired "): A flattering nickname given to Louis XVI, King of France, on his accession in 1774.

DIET: Name used in the Germanic countries for a Deliberative Assembly. Equals Senate; or sometimes, Parliament.

EMPIRE, GERMAN (*see* CHARLEMAGNE): Napoleon annexed North Germany to France; and made his generals Kings of Holland, Würtemburg, etc.

" ELEVEN MEN " (referred to on page 10): The provisional Government of the French Republic inaugurated by the Revolution of February 1848; Dupont de l'Eure, Alphonse de Lavartise, Gaston Crémieux, Etiénne Arago, Ledru Rollin, Garnier Pages, Manart, Flocon, Louis Blanc and Albert.

FOURIER, FRANÇOIS MARIE CHARLES (1772-1837): Leading French Utopian Socialist. His followers formed a dogmatic sect who opposed all class struggle as such.

FRANCIS I: Emperor (of Austria) from 1792 to 1835; was the first to use the title Emperor of Austria, renouncing the older style of " Germano-Roman " Emperor in 1804.

FREDERICK WILLIAM IV: King of Prussia from 1840 to 1861; was a believer in the " divine right of kings " and addicted to a mystic pietism; certified insane in 1857.

FROEBEL: German democratic politician; delegate with Robert Blum from the Frankfurt National Assembly to Vienna; not to be confused with the celebrated educationist.

GERMAN CATHOLICS: A " breakaway " from the Catholic Church, led by a Silesian priest (Rouge) who denounced the exhibition of the " Holy Coat " at Truro as idolatry. The movement soon included over 300 congregations. After the Revolution it was roughly handled by the Government and died away.

GLOSSARY

GERMANY, YOUNG (*see* "YOUNG GERMANY").

HANSEMANN, DAVID JUSTUS LUDWIG (1790-1864): Prussian banker and Liberal politician.

HAYNAU, JULIUS JAKOB, BARON VON (1780-1858): Austrian General notorious for the savagery of his suppression of the Italian revolt, 1848-9, and especially for ordering the flogging of women after the capture of Brescia—in revenge for which he was horsewhipped by the draymen of Barclay's Brewery when he visited it in 1850. Appointed Dictator of Hungary in 1849, but was dismissed from the post a few months later.

HEINE, HEINRICH (1799-1856) "The greatest German poet since Goethe and the wittiest Frenchman since Voltaire." Born in Düsseldorf of Jewish parents he died in Paris—having been crippled and agonised with spinal paralysis since early in 1848. Until his illness played an important part in discrediting the reactionary authorities by the inimitable skill of his satire, which caused the censor to forbid publication in advance to anything he might write. An intimate friend of Marx and Engels.

IN PARTIBUS INFIDELIUM: "in parts possessed by the Infidels," term used by the Papacy for countries where the Catholic religion is not officially recognised by the State; here used in derision of countries still in the hands of Kings and Aristocracy to which the Republican chiefs had to fly for refuge.

JELLACHICH, JOSEPH, BARON (1801-59): Austrian General, appointed "Ban" (or "Headman") of the Croats in 1848; as such led the Croats to the side of the Hapsburg Emperor against Vienna and Hungary.

JOSEPH II (1741-90): Became Emperor in 1765, but his power was restricted until the death of his mother Maria-Theresa in 1780. Thereafter pursued an expansionist policy and instigated the partitions of Poland between Russia, Austria and Prussia. Quarrelled with the Papacy and forbade the circulation of Papal decrees without his prior sanction. Aimed at being a "Grand Monarch."

LANDWEHR: The conscript militia-reserve.

GLOSSARY

LEDRU-ROLLIN, ALEXANDRE AUGUSTE (1807-74): Lawyer, leader of the Democratic Republicans in France; advocate of universal suffrage; member of the Provisional Government of February 1848; lost prestige along with that Government by its suppression of the proletariat in June 1848; himself attempted an insurrection in 1849 and was exiled until 1870.

LEGITIMISTS: The Party supporting the claims to Restoration of the Older Bourbon Monarchy overthrown in 1792 and again in 1830.

LIEUTENANT, GERMAN IMPERIAL: The official title of the Regent, Archduke John of Austria, appointed by the Frankfurt Parliament with Imperial sanction.

LOUIS PHILIPPE, King of the French (1773-1850): As Duke of Orleans was elected King after the bourgeois Revolution of July 1830; was deposed by the Revolution of February 1848. Died in England.

LUSATIA: An ancient German territory to the north of Bohemia —of which it originally formed part; annexed by Saxony it was in 1815 divided, the northern part going to Saxony, the southern to Prussia.

MAINE LIQUOR LAW: The State of Maine, U.S.A., in 1851 passed a law prohibiting the manufacture, sale or use of intoxicating liquor.

MANIFESTO, THE: The " Manifesto of the Communist Party," by Karl Marx and Frederick Engels.

MANTEUFFE, OTTO VON: Prussian statesman; signed the treaty between Prussia and Austria at Olmütz in 1850.

MARRAST, ARMAND (1801-52): French journalist and politician; editor of the *National*, member of the Provisional Government 1848; President of the National Assembly.

MESSENHAUSER: Leader of the Vienna insurrection of October 1848; ex-soldier, popular orator and journalist, member of the Reichstag; an honest and courageous man; executed after the defeat of the rising.

GLOSSARY 153

METTERNICH, CLEMENS, LOTHAR WENZEL, PRINCE (1773-1859): Took a leading part in the Congress of Vienna; from 1815 was the most representative reactionary in Europe; was Austrian Imperial Chancellor from 1815 till the Revolution of March 1848.

" MODERN SCHOOL ": (see " YOUNG GERMANY ").

MIEROSLAWSKI, LUDWIG VON: Polish general sentenced to death for activity in the Cracow insurrection of 1846; amnested and released at the demand of the revolutionaries in Berlin, March 1848; raised an insurrection in Posen, May 1848; gained a victory for the Baden insurrection in June 1849 but was defeated in the subsequent battles and at the end of June threw up his command.

" NEUE RHEINISCHE ZEITUNG ": Journal founded by Karl Marx in Cologne, May 1848; it was denounced by Reactionaries and Liberals alike; after the Prussian *coup d'état* in November it published at the head of every issue an appeal to refuse to pay taxes and to meet force by force; for this it was twice persecuted —on the first occasion the accused were Marx, Engels and Korff; on the second they were Marx, Schapper and Schneider. Charged with " inciting the people to armed resistance against the Government," Marx conducted the defence and secured a unanimous acquittal—" at the end of the trial the jurors sent to thank him for his instructive lecture." The paper, which during its run, had been contributed to by Marx, Engels, W. Wolff, Werth, Lassalle and Freiligrath, was finally suppressed, May 19th, 1849; its final issue was one sustained defiance; printed in red ink! Lenin called the *Neue Rheinische Zeitung* " a model of revolutionary journalism."

PENATES: Household gods among the Romans.

QUIXOTE, DON: Cervantes' novel of that name, burlesque of feudal romanticism in the figure of a noble-natured old knight who has crazed himself by reading romances and in his search for adventure meets nothing but grotesque mishaps.

RADETZKY, JOHANN JOSEPH, COUNT (1766-1858): Austrian general; commander-in-chief in Lombardy from 1831; after the defeat of the insurrection of 1848 ruled the territory of Lombardy-Venetia with " an iron hand." Died in Milan while still in command.

RHENISH GAZETTE: Founded in 1842 as the organ of the liberal bourgeoisie of the Rhineland. On leaving the university Marx became first a contributor and then editor of the paper. His radical views proved too much for the owners and the Prussian Government and in 1843 he had to resign and emigrate to Paris.

SCHWARTZENBURG, FELIX, LUDWIG JOHANN FRIEDERICH, PRINCE (1800-52): Austrian soldier and diplomat; appointed Prime Minister in 1848 he called in the Russians to aid in the defeat of the Hungarian insurgents.

SIGEL, FRANZ: Second in command of the Baden insurrection, took over command after Mieroslawski's resignation; effected an escape into Switzerland with the remnant of his army; served with distinction on the Northern side in the American Civil War.

ST. SIMON, CLAUDE HENRI, CONTE DE (1760-1825): Founder of Utopian Socialism in France; opposed the " positive reorganisation of society " to what he regarded as " destructive revolution." In spite of his limitations St. Simon was a powerful critic of capitalist society.

TRIBUNE, THE NEW YORK DAILY: Newspaper founded by Horace Greeley, celebrated humanitarian, sympathetic to (Utopian) Socialism; of Liberal tendencies. For many years the most popular and widely read paper in North America. Marx's sole regular income for years was the £1 a week received for his weekly political letter to the *Tribune*. Many of these letters were in fact (as were those which constitute this work) written by Engels.

VENDÉE: District on the west coast of France, notorious as the centre of a pro-Royalist insurrection of rich peasants and former landlords against the French Republic in 1793. From this association the name is extended to any agrarian clerical-royalist counter-revolutionary movement.

VIENNA, CONGRESS OF: (*see* " CONGRESS ").

GLOSSARY

Vogt, Karl (1817-95): Naturalist, Professor at Giessen, dismissed from the post as a revolutionist in 1847; prominent in the Frankfurt Parliament; later became a Bonapartist secret agent and as such was exposed in Marx's pamphlet *Herr Vogt*. Vogt was the most famous exponent of so-called "vulgar" materialism, that is of a mechanical, non-dialectical materialist philosophy.

Welder, Karl Theodor (1790-1869): Publicist and politician; in 1848 Professor at Freiburg; from 1834-44 was editor, with Rotteck, of the *Staatslexicon*.

Windischgrätz, Prince (1788-62): Austrian field-marshal; suppressed the revolution of 1848-9 in Prague and Vienna, after a number of victories over the Hungarians was defeated by them at Gordolboz and consequently relieved of his command.

Wrangel, Friederich Heinrich Ernst (1784-1877): Prussian Field-Marshal; served in the Napoleonic wars and in those against Schleswig-Holstein, Denmark, and Austria—as well as suppressing the revolution in Berlin, 1848.

Wolff, Wilhelm (1809-64): Karl Marx, dedicated the first volume of *Capital* to "my never-to-be-forgotten friend, the brave, true, noble, fighter in the vanguard of the Proletariat, Wilhelm Wolff." He died in exile at Manchester.

Young Germany: A school of writers (of whom the best known was Heine) denounced by special decree of the Federal Diet in 1835. This decree stated that "the declared aim" of this school was "to attack the Christian religion in the most insolent manner, to bring existing institutions into contempt, and to subvert all discipline and morality." The States of Germany were enjoined to enforce the criminal law and the police regulations against this school "with the greatest stringency."

Zollverein: literally "Customs Unions," an agreement among the Western States of the German Confederation to adopt simultaneously free trade among themselves and a common tariff against all goods from outside the group.